Physical Characteristics of the English Cocker Spaniel

(from the American Kennel C

Body: Compact and well-knit, giving the impression of

Back: Short and strong.

Tail: Docked. Set on to conform to croup.

Hindquarters: Angulation moderate and, most importantly, in balance with that of the forequarters.

Color: Various. Parti-colors are either clearly marked, ticked or roaned, the white appearing in combination with black, liver or shades of red. Solid colors are black, liver or shades of red.

Height at withers: Males, 16 to 17 inches; females, 15 to 16 inches.

Weight: Males, 28 to 34 pounds; females, 26 to 32 pounds.

Feet: Proportionate in size to the legs, firm, round and catlike; toes arched and tight; pads thick.

English Cocker Spaniel

◇

By Haja van Wessem

Contents

Training Your English Cocker Spaniel 81

Begin with the basics of training the puppy and adult dog. Learn the principles of house-training the English Cocker Spaniel, including the use of crates and basic scent instincts. Get started by introducing the pup to his collar and leash and progress to the basic commands. Find out about obedience classes and other activities.

Healthcare of Your English Cocker Spaniel 102

By Lowell Ackerman, DVM, DACVD
Become your dog's healthcare advocate and a well-educated canine keeper. Select a skilled and able veterinarian. Discuss pet insurance, vaccinations and infectious diseases, breed-specific hereditary concerns, the neuter/spay decision and a sensible, effective plan for parasite control, including fleas, ticks and worms.

Showing Your English Cocker Spaniel 132

Step into the center ring and find out about the world of showing pure-bred dogs. Acquaint yourself with the basics of AKC conformation showing and explore other areas of canine competition: obedience, agility, tracking and field and hunting events.

Behavior of Your English Cocker Spaniel 144

Analyze the canine mind to understand what makes your English Cocker Spaniel tick. The potential problems discussed include aggression, dominance, separation anxiety, chewing, barking, begging and more.

KENNEL CLUB BOOKS® ENGLISH COCKER SPANIEL
ISBN: 1-59378-208-X

Copyright © 2005 • Kennel Club Books, LLC
308 Main Street, Allenhurst, NJ 07711 USA
Cover Design Patented: US 6,435,559 B2 • Printed in South Korea

Photography by:

Paulette Braun, T.J. Calhoun, Alan and Sandy Carey, Carolina Biological Supply, Isabelle Français, Carol Ann Johnson, Bill Jonas, Dr. Dennis Kunkel, Tam C. Nguyen, Phototake, Jean Claude Revy, Haja van Wessem and Derek Whitehouse.

Illustrations by Renée Low and Patricia Peters.

The publisher wishes to thank all of the owners whose dogs are illustrated in this book.

It is believed that spaniels, as a general dog type, were identified more than 2,500 years ago. One theory puts forth that the word "spaniel" derived from the Carthaginian word for "rabbit."

ENGLISH COCKER SPANIEL

EARLY SPANIEL HISTORY

In 500 B.C. when the Carthaginians landed in Spain during one of their travels in the Mediterranean, the soldiers saw a great number of rabbits and they shouted "Span, span!" (*span* being the Carthaginian word for "rabbit"). Thus the land was called *Hispania*, or "rabbit-land," and the dogs that they saw in pursuit of the rabbits became known as *spaniels* or "rabbit-dogs."

Is this how spaniels got their name? Or is it the fantasy of Virginia Woolf, who tells us this delightful little story in her book *Flush*, the biography of Elizabeth Barrett Browning's spaniel. It is very likely that the spaniel lived in the countries surrounding the Mediterranean and thus in Spain. He might have gotten his name through the Basque word *Espana*; the fact that there are several spaniel-like breeds in France that are called *épagneuls* also points in this direction.

The fact is that the spaniel can be considered to be one of the oldest dog types in history. In the Metropolitan Museum in New York a small statue in terracotta can be seen that has a decidedly spaniel-like appearance. The statue is over 2,000 years old and belongs to the Cypriot Collection.

More proof of the antiquity of the breed can be seen from the first mention of a spaniel in the early Irish Laws in a statement that water spaniels had been given as a tribute to the king. Spaniels also traveled to Wales, where they were the treasured dogs of King Hywel Dha (Howell

A 2,000-year-old terracotta (clay) figure of an early spaniel-type dog. Historians of many breeds rely on ancient artifacts to substantiate the relative antiquity of a type of dog.

the Good). The king's love for his spaniels went so far that the dogs received a special mention in one of the laws of the country in 948 A.D. At this time, for the price of one spaniel, a person could buy a number of goats, women, slaves or geese! In these laws, mammals are divided into birds, beasts and dogs, and the "dogs" classification was subdivided into tracker, greyhound and spaniel.

The first mention of a spaniel in English literature comes as early as Chaucer (ca. 1340–1400) and Gaston de Foix, who died in 1391. Chaucer, author of *The Canterbury Tales*, refers to the spaniel several times ("for as a Spaynel she wol on hym lepe"), which proves

beyond doubt that the spaniel was known in England 600 years ago. Gaston de Foix mentions the spaniel in his work *Miroir de Phoebus* or, as it is also known, *Livre de Chasse*. Gaston de Foix was a feudal baron who lived in France near the Spanish border, and he was convinced that Spain was the country of origin of the spaniel. "Another manner of hound there is, called hounds for the hawk, and Spaniels, for their kind came from Spain, notwithstanding that there be many in other countries. Such hounds have many good customs and evil. Also a fair hound for the hawk should have a great head, a great body, and be of fair hue, white or tawny (i.e., pied, speckled or mottled), for they be fairest and of such hue they be commonly the best." He then describes them as being "hounds [the word *dog* was not used then] with a great head and a great, strong body. Their color is red and white of orange roan, but black and white can also be seen. They run and wag their tail and raise or start fowl and wild beasts. Their right craft is the partridge and the quail. They can also be taught to take partridge and quail with the net and they love to swim."

Another early reference to "Spanyellys" occurs in *The Boke of St. Albans* (1486), also named *The Book of Field Sports*,

CANIS LUPUS
"Grandma, what big teeth you have!" The gray wolf, a familiar figure in fairy tales and legends, has had its reputation tarnished and its population pummeled over the centuries. Yet it is the descendants of this much-feared creature to which we open our homes and hearts. Our beloved dog, *Canis domesticus*, derives directly from the gray wolf, a highly social canine that lives in elaborately structured packs. In the wild, the gray wolf can range from 60 to 175 pounds, standing between 25 and 40 inches in height.

written by Dame Juliana Berners, prioress of Sopwell Nunnery, Hertfordshire. It is obviously a school book and it is assumed that the book was written for the use of the royal princes, to teach them to read and make them acquainted with the names of the animals and phrases used in hunting and field sports.

In the book there is frequent mention of spaniels in the royal household. Thus we read that "Robin, the King's Majesty's Spaniel Keeper" was paid a certain sum for "hair cloth to rub the Spaniels with."

NETTING

In the days of Henry VIII, the many banquets called for large amounts of food, of which game was an important part. Game such as partridge, quail, pheasant, rabbit and hare was caught in snares, but because of the never-ending demand, a more speedy method of catching the game was sought. This method was found in "netting." Spaniels were used to drive the birds towards the fowlers, who stood ready with their extended nets. Dog and bird were caught under the net. The spaniels that were used for this kind of work were called "sitting" or "setting" spaniels, and they are the ancestors of our modern setters.

In his book *Treatise of Englishe Dogges* (1570) Dr.

Johannes Caius (pseudonym for John Keyes) described the way that the dogs are taught to let themselves be caught under the net. Dr. Caius classified all sporting dogs under two headings: *Venatici*, used for the purpose of hunting beasts, and *Aucupatorii*, used for the hunting of fowl. He subdivided this latter group into "Setters which findeth game on the land" and "Spaniells which findeth game on the water." He named this group *Hispaniolus*. He also was of the opinion that these dogs originated in Spain. He described them as white with red markings and—be it more rare— red or black, and he gave a special mention to a dog brought in from France in 1570 that was "speckled all over with white and black,

PURPOSEFUL PAIRINGS

It was only in the 19th century that humans really took notice of the dogs around them: how they looked, what color they were and how tall they were. Dogs all along have been helpmates—some dogs killed vermin and some dogs protected the property. Breeding a certain dog to a certain bitch was not necessarily accidental. More than likely, humans paired dogs for their abilities. To produce a dog for a specific purpose, they would mate two dogs with the qualities needed for that purpose. Thus were progenerated various dogs with superior abilities.

PURE-BRED PURPOSE

Given the vast range of the world's 400 or so pure breeds of dog, it's fair to say that domestic dogs are the most versatile animal in the kingdom. From the tiny 1-pound lap dog to the 200-pound guard dog, dogs have adapted to every need and whim of their human masters. Humans have selectively bred dogs to alter physical attributes like size, color, leg length, mass and skull diameter in order to suit our own needs and fancies. Dogs serve humans as companions and guardians as well as hunters, exterminators, shepherds, rescuers, messengers, warriors, babysitters and more!

which mingled color incline to a marble blue which beautifieth their skins and affordeth a seemly show of comliness." That, undoubtedly, was the first blue roan spaniel!

In the 16th and 17th centuries another group of spaniels was recognized: the Toy Spaniel. Since the Toy Spaniel in those days was bigger and heavier in build than our modern Toy Spaniels, it is very likely that there was a relationship between the Blenheim Spaniel and King Charles Spaniel and the hunting spaniels. Moreover, it wasn't unusual for Blenheim Spaniels to be used in the field.

The English Springer Spaniel, shown here, is a completely distinct breed from the English Cocker Spaniel, though both breeds share common ancestors and shared a revival in the US.

THE FIRST COCKERS

With the invention of the gun, netting disappeared and the game was caught by shooting. The setting spaniels were used to find the game and point it so that it could be shot, and the springing spaniels had to flush the game from the cover.

In *The Sportsman's Cabinet,* written by Nicolas Cox and published in 1803, we find a description of the spaniel: "The race of dogs passing under the denomination of spaniels are of two kinds, one of which is considerably larger than the other, and are known by the appellation of the springing spaniel—as applicable to every kind of game in every country: the smaller is called the cocker or cocking spaniel, as being more adapted to covert and woodcock shooting, to which they are more particularly appropriated and by nature seem designed." We may assume, therefore, that the Cocker Spaniel derives his name from the woodcock or, as some believe, the cockpheasant. Cox continues to give a description of the Cocker who "has a shorter, more compact form, a rounder head, shorter nose, ears long (and the longer the more admired), the limbs short and strong, the coat more inclined to curl than the springers, is longer, particularly on the tail, which is generally truncated; color liver-and-white, red, red-

and-white, black-and-white, all liver color and not infrequently black with tanned legs and muzzle." From the great similitude between some of these English Cockers and the small water-dogs, both in figure and disposition, there is little doubt but they may have been originally produced by a cross between the springing spaniel and the latter.

The English Cocker is, again, praised for his rapid action in the field, his tireless enthusiasm in finding and pursuing hare or in

Eng. Ch. Wribbenenhall Waiter, a turn-of-the-century champion Field Spaniel, was considered an excellent example of the correct Field Spaniel in those days. Excessively long and low dogs were out of fashion because they were inferior workers in the field.

searching winged game. His tail is mentioned as "being in perpetual motion," a feature that, fortunately, has been preserved in our modern English Cockers with their ever-wagging tails.

In the course of the 19th century we see a new variety of spaniel emerge: the Field Spaniel. The main difference between the Field and the Cocker is weight. The Field Spaniel was a strong black dog whose weight should exceed 25 pounds; otherwise, he would be classified as a Cocker. The fact that pups from the same litter could be classified as different breeds, either Cocker or Field, was detrimental to both breeds and, where the popularity of the Field Spaniel was increasing all the time, the future of the Cocker didn't look too good. The decision of England's

still to be found in the pedigrees of our modern English Cockers. It was also Mr. James Farrow who, in 1902, founded the Cocker Spaniel Club of Great Britain (in England, the breed is called simply Cocker Spaniel), which is still going strong today. Also in 1902, The Kennel Club issued the first official breed standard.

Fred and Eng. Ch. Obo, born in June 1879, were bred by Mr. James Farrow, who laid the foundation for the English Cocker Spaniel breed.

Kennel Club to recognize them as different breeds probably saved the Cocker from extinction. Fields and Cockers were both seen at shows and the Cocker began to make steady progress.

HISTORY OF THE BREED IN ITS HOMELAND

It was undoubtedly Mr. James Farrow who built the foundation for the breed as we know it today. He bred the original Obo, who was born on June 14, 1879. Mr. Farrow's Bob Obo was the forerunner of the modern English Cocker Spaniel. Names such as Eng. Ch. Ted Obo and Tim Obo are

A contemporary of Mr. Farrow was Mr. C.A. Phillips, originator of the Rivington strain. He bred black and colored English Cockers that all came from Obo stock. Mr. Phillips had a particular interest in the working side of the English Cocker, and he helped promote field trials in the beginning of this century. He himself was a very successful competitor and bred many field trial champions, of whom Rivington Simon, Rivington Rogue and Rivington Reine are probably the best known.

In 1875 Mr. R. Lloyd founded his Of Ware strain that later

Field Trial
Champion
Rivington Sam,
born in 1911, bred
by Mr. C. A.
Phillips, shown in a
painting by R.
Ward Binks.

proved to be so incredibly influential. The name "Of Ware" was not introduced by Mr. R. Lloyd but by his son H.S. Lloyd, who carried on the kennel after the death of his father. Famous Of Ware dogs were the Champions Invader of Ware, Whoopee of Ware and Exquisite of Ware, to be followed by many, many others in later years. The influence of Mr. Lloyd's dogs remained strong until long after World War II.

Another kennel that must be mentioned because of its success and its influence on the history of the breed is the Bowdler kennel of Mr. R. de Courcy Peele, founded in 1898. Eng. Ch. Ben Bowdler ex Judy Bowdler produced Eng. Ch. Bob Bowdler; Judy Bowdler was also the dam of Eng. Ch. Rufus Bowdler. From

Jetsam Bowdler and Jock Bowdler came Rocklyn Magic, a dog that is featured in so many pedigrees and who was a very good producer.

Braeside Bustle is a name that is familiar to many fanciers. He was born in 1894 and was the sire of Blue Peter, a dog that had a remarkable influence in fixing and transmitting the characteristics of the colored variety. Another son of Braeside Bustle was the aforementioned Eng. Ch. Ben Bowdler. Most of our colored English Cockers trace back to this wonderful sire, Braeside Bustle. Owner of the Braeside Cockers was Mr. J.M. Porter.

During World War I (1914–1918) all breeding activities stopped, but after the war a few dedicated breeders succeeded in restoring the breed and the

Luckystar of Ware, a blue roan, was the Supreme Champion of the UK's prestigious Crufts show in 1930 and 1931. This dog was considered by many to have been the greatest of all English Cockers in his day.

Braeside Bustle sired such champions as Ben Bowdler and Blue Peter. These are all great names in the history of the English Cocker breed.

Rocklyn Magic, who features in so many influential pedigrees, descended from the well-known Bowdler breeding.

English Cocker became more popular than ever in the field as well as in the show ring. The conditions in the field, however, changed and English Cockers were asked to retrieve. To be able to retrieve a dog must be in balance, and balance requires a strong neck and a short back. For the longcast, low-legged English Cocker with a comparatively short neck, this new task proved to be impossible and breeders began to aim for a more square, leggier and shorter-backed dog. It was this variety that traveled around the

world—Europe, India, South Africa, Australia, China, Canada and New Zealand.

Influential breeders of the period between 1918 and 1940 were Mrs. A.H. Gold of Oxshotts, whose homebred Eng. Ch. Oxshott Marxedes was a famous sire; Mrs. Judy de Casembroot of Treetops, who succeeded in establishing a line of very successful and very homogeneous blacks, of which

Treetops Walkie Talkie is probably best remembered; and Mrs. Veronica Lucas-Lucas, who established her Sixshot kennel in the 1930s, starting with blacks and reds but later also including parti-colors. Sixshots Black Swan is said to have been of extreme influence to the solid English Cockers of today.

The Broomleaf kennel, founded by Mrs. Kay Doxford, was to become a powerful force for good red and black English Cockers. Her Eng. Ch. Broomleaf Bonny Lad of Shillwater not only won 15 Challenge Certificates but also qualified in the field and

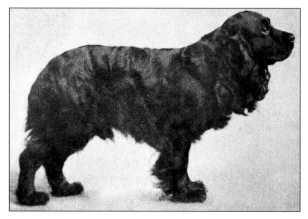

proved to be a very good stud dog.

In those years between the two wars, English Cockers did extremely well. The breed was popular and flourishing, culminating with the Best in Show wins of Eng. Sh. Ch. Luckystar of Ware at the 1930 and 1931 Crufts Dog Shows. This success was repeated in 1938 and 1939 by Eng. Sh. Ch. Exquisite Model of Ware and again in 1948 and 1950 (there was no Crufts in 1949) when Eng. Sh. Ch. Tracy Witch of Ware became Supreme Best in Show at Crufts.

Together with Lorna Countess Howe, Mr. H.S. Lloyd is the only one to succeed in winning a Best in Show twice in a row at Crufts—and he did it three times! No breeder since has been so successful. In 1970 Mrs. Joyce Caddy came close when her Ch. Ouaine Chieftain won Reserve Best in Show, and in 1996 Mrs. Patricia Bentley's Caniou Cambrai won Best in Show.

The famed Broomleaf kennel, founded by Mrs. Kay Doxford, produced some wonderful dogs, as exemplified by Eng. Ch. Broomleaf Bonny Lad of Shillwater.

World War II again put a stop to all breeding, and many breeders had their entire stock put down, out of fear of an invasion. Whereas during the 1914–1918 war dog showing continued, this was not the case in World War II. At the end of the war breeders tentatively started to breed again and as the demand for puppies grew, more breeding was undertaken. Mr. H.S. Lloyd still carried on and although he had a smaller number of dogs, he still had a small team of stud dogs on which breeders greatly relied.

New people came into the breed and a new star, rising very quickly, was the Lochranza kennel of Miss Macmillan and Miss

A famous English Cocker, featured in many of the pedigrees of champion dogs, is Eng. Ch. Oxshott Marxedes, bred by Mrs. A. H. Gold.

Charles. Dogs from their breeding that will always be remembered are Eng. Sh. Ch. Lochranza Dancing Master, Lochranza Merryleaf Eiger, Eng. Sh. Ch. Lochranza Strollaway and many, many others.

Coming into the 1950s, we find that this decade can be qualified as the vintage for English Cocker Spaniels. Many of the old established kennels continued to bring out dogs and bitches of great quality, and kennels that had started during or after the war became big names in their own right. One of those pre-war kennels that built up strongly after 1948 was the Colinwood kennel of Mr. A.W. Collins. In nearly every pedigree of modern English Cockers we can find the tri-color Eng. Ch. Colinwood Cowboy, who had a tremendous influence on the breed, as well as Eng. Sh. Ch. Colinwood Silver Lariot. Mr. Alf Collins died in the 1960s after having been in the breed for about 40 years. He left the kennel and the Colinwood prefix to his daughter, Mrs. Woolf, who had been as keenly involved in the Colinwood English Cockers as he was and who is still active as a breeder and a judge today.

The Craigleith English Cockers, founded by Mrs. Mollie Robinson, are worth a mention. She produced some of the top winners, not only in Great Britain but also in many other countries, notably the United States and South Africa.

In 1963 the English Cocker Spaniel world suffered a great loss with the death of Mr. H. S. Lloyd, but fortunately his daughter Jennifer, who shared his love for

English Cockers, carries on with the famous Of Ware and Falconers prefixes.

The first dog to be registered with the Scolys prefix was Scolys Simon in 1955, bred by Mrs. Dilys Schofield. She bred several champions, at home and overseas, but her most famous one is Eng. Sh. Ch. Scolys Starduster, who not only was considered to be the prototype for the standard but who also was a great sire of winners. He is by another dog that turned out to be very influential, Eng. Sh. Ch. Goldenfields Minstrel Boy.

Nowadays the breed is still prospering. There are a great number of dedicated breeders and at the shows we see many English Cockers of great quality.

THE ENGLISH COCKER SPANIEL IN AMERICA

The history of the English Cocker Spaniel in America is a very interesting one. Few Americans

are aware that from the worldwide perspective, the more well-known Cocker Spaniel is the English variety. Outside the United States there are Cocker Spaniels and American Cocker Spaniels, whereas in the United States there are Cocker Spaniels and English Cocker Spaniels!

In the 1870s there were quite a number of breeders of Field Spaniels and Cocker Spaniels and, as in England, the dividing line between the two breeds was the weight. The Cocker limit was around 28 pounds; anything above that was a Field Spaniel. This situation changed when in 1884 a couple of Obo sons arrived in utero from England. Mr. Farrow had sent the bitch Chloe II, in whelp by Ch. Obo, over to Mr. F.F. Fletcher. One of these puppies, Obo II, was sold to Mr. J.P. Wiley,

An important sire, well respected as a top producer, was Eng. Sh. Ch. Courtdale Flag Lieutenant. The dog was bred by Mrs. D. Schofield of Scolys kennel.

Eng. Sh. Ch. Colinwood Silver Lariot had a tremendous influence on the breed.

and this dog proved to be as prepotent as his famous sire. What Obo II did for the breed in the United States was as important as what his sire Obo did in England—they managed to establish weight and type in the breed. Interest in the breed in the 1890s became very keen and the breed thrived.

However, gradually it appeared that the English Cockers were becoming smaller in size and that some of them looked more like toy dogs. The new standard, published in 1901, did nothing to help that situation—it accepted the English Cockers as they were and it did not encourage the development of a stronger, more workmanlike type of dog. Mr. Wiley, whose kennel had been so important in the first years, tried to cross with Field Spaniels. When that did not give

There were many beautiful Lochranza English Cockers, but Eng. Sh. Ch. Lochranza Strollaway was undoubtedly one of the best.

HEALTH AND THE ECSCA

Along with holding specialty shows, promoting breeding ethics and generally safeguarding the breed in the US, one of the main functions of the English Cocker Spaniel Club of America is to help fund health research in the breed. Throughout the decades, they have partnered with other organizations to advance health studies, with the goal of pinpointing hereditary issues in the breed and determining how to eliminate them from the breed. Eye disease has always been a focus in the English Cocker, as well as hip dysplasia. Today, another main hereditary concern is familial nephropathy, a condition that causes kidney failure at a young age.

---

him the results he wanted, he eventually retired, much to the regret of all English Cocker fanciers.

Obviously something had to be done. The tendency toward a decrease in size, the domed skulls and the round eyes were clearly an inheritance of the King Charles Spaniel blood, introduced at an earlier period. The English Cocker became so refined and beautiful that its classification in the Sporting Group was largely a matter of toleration and was being frequently questioned.

However, we have to thank the Sporting Spaniel Society for saving the English Cocker from becoming a toy dog and the

Springer Spaniel from becoming extinct. These breeders set out, with the material they had—the liver-and-white and black-and-white Keeper's Spaniels, the Clumbers, the old English Water Spaniels, the Sussex Spaniels and the setter/spaniel crosses that were owned by sportsmen—to develop the Springer Spaniel. With this breeding they created,

as a by-product, an English Cocker that was as closely related to the modern Springer as the original English Cocker was related to the Field Spaniel. This could well be the explanation of why so many pedigrees of English Cockers cannot be traced back to Obo II, whereas so many pedigrees of American Cockers can.

Around 1910 the breeders realized that the two types, the English and the American, were no longer compatible, and importing all but stopped. At that time, however, England had developed the more modern

Winner of the World Show in Frankfurt, Germany in 1935 was Woodcock's Memory, an English Cocker shown by Mrs. L. van Herwaarden of Holland.

English Cocker, the shorter-backed, leggier version, and in the late 1920s these Cockers began to appear in the United States in increasing numbers. This dog, being so different from what the American Cocker fanciers considered ideal, could not compete in the show ring with the American dogs, and attempts to incorporate its qualities in the well-established American Cocker were met with unwillingness.

It was thanks to Mr. E. Shippen Willing, a dedicated fancier of the British type, and Mr. Russell H. Johnson Jr., president of the American Kennel Club, that this British type was recognized by the American Kennel Club and was given

Ch. Obo II, founder of English Cocker Spaniel lineage in the United States. Although he looks long and low by modern-day standards, he was considered more functional in type than his forebears. He was bred to no fewer than 72 bitches in the US and Canada.

Mepals Rosemary was an early American Cocker Spaniel.

classes at the shows in 1936, the same year as the formation of the English Cocker Spaniel Club of America (ECSCA). From that moment on, the English Cocker Spaniel developed rapidly. Quality English Cockers from Great Britain, Holland and Germany were imported and the breed started to establish itself in its own right until World War II put an end to that. Imports stopped, breeding slowed down, dog showing decreased. Mrs. Geraldine R. Dodge, one of the earliest fanciers of the breed, used this relatively quiet period of time to prove that the two varieties were actually separate breeds. She proved that they had been bred separately for more than the five generations required and she rewrote the standard for the English Cocker, making it sufficiently different from the

standard for the American breed so that there might be less confusion. She succeeded in 1946 when the two breeds were officially separated and the American Kennel Club recognized the English Cocker Spaniel as a breed. While the American Cocker remains one of the most popular breeds in the United States, the English Cocker is now also firmly established here.

Following the division of the two Cockers into separate breeds, in the US there were the Cocker Spaniel (the US's name for the American variety, which is known as American Cocker Spaniel elsewhere in the world) and the English Cocker Spaniel. Obviously there were separate breed standards, and the AKC English Cocker standard differed from the UK standard. One difference was (and still is) that slightly taller dogs are allowed in the US, but there are other differences,

too, which still exist today.

Many of the early successful dogs were British imports. Mrs. Dodge continued to be an influential figure in the breed, owning some top dogs and even holding breed specialty shows on the grounds of her home. Another prominent figure was Mrs. Anne Rogers Clark of the Surrey prefix; Mrs. Rogers Clark's involvement in dogs has been a lifelong pursuit, and today she is one of the world's most respected judges.

The 1950s and '60s saw some important English Cockers, most of them imported from the UK or bred in the US from British bloodlines. While the breed's overall numbers declined, two very important kennels made an impression that would reach far into future decades. Maple Lawn and Soho kennels were in their prime and these lines are seen still in today's pedigrees.

Some record-making dogs of the 1970s include Ch. Kenobo Capricorn, who still heads the list as the all-time top-producing sire in the breed. "Goat," as he was called, was owned by Bonnie Threlfall and bred by Helga Tustin, and was also a Best in Show, multiple Group and specialty show winner, even winning a specialty at eight years of age. Ch. Applewyn of Angus gained fame for earning his championship before nine months of age, achieving his first Group

A beautiful American-bred English Cocker Spaniel.

win before he was one year old; he became a top producer.

In the late 1970s, the English Cocker was permitted to enter working tests held by the English Springer Spaniel club and Cockers started to earn titles. From the 1980s to the present, there have been many important names and kennels making their mark on the English Cocker breed. Barbara Heckerman was a well-known handler of many top-winning dogs, as well as a breeder under her Wyncrest prefix. In addition to the newer kennels, other names that figure prominently in the breed today are some of the top names of yesteryear, including Dunelm, Wittersham, Lochranza, Braeside, Ranzfel and many more.

ENGLISH COCKER PERSONALITY

If we look at the AKC breed standard, the first words that strike us are "active," "merry" and "sporting." The standard of the breed's homeland describes the English Cocker as "merry, sturdy and sporting." There's no denying it, these things are the essence of an English Cocker Spaniel, and the fact that the standards open with these words may well indicate their importance. An English Cocker Spaniel is a happy dog—happy with you and with the family, but also with complete strangers and other dogs. He is happy to work and happy to play; he is the ultimate optimist. He gets up every morning with the joyful expectation of another lovely day, with lots of fun, hopefully a lot to eat (because he loves his food!) and who knows what new and exciting adventures! He will follow you around in the house; he wants to know what you are doing and he would hate to miss any of the fun and excitement. He loves to share his happiness with everybody, and if this means that he jumps up on you with four muddy paws, then you have to accept that in the sense with which it was done! His happy, easygoing temperament also makes him a fatalist. If he cannot come with you he will express his great sorrow (and he can look very sorrowful!), but he will accept the situation and make the best of it. If his feet are to be trimmed he will try to wriggle out of it, but if you are firm he will give a mental shrug and go

A good English Cocker should be merry, sturdy and sporting. Above all, he must be a happy dog.

to sleep on the grooming table. However, this behavior makes it very important that you are gentle but firm with him because he is clever enough to realize that when he gets his way once, he may get it again, and again...

Sometimes we come across an English Cocker with a bad temperament. It should be the duty of breeders not to breed from an English Cocker with either an aggressive or a nervous temperament. Unfortunately, this does not always happen, and it is the unfortunate puppy buyer who has to face the consequences. Investigations are still going on to find out whether bad temperament is a hereditary problem or not. So far, the problem has mainly occurred in solids. It is of the utmost importance that you buy a puppy from a breeder with a good reputation and preferably one whose dogs you have met. If you know that temperament problems have occurred more than once in a certain line, you would do well to avoid this line. Anything other than a happy personality is atypical of the breed and *not* a trait that should be perpetuated.

Although an English Cocker thinks that every guest to your house has been invited especially to please him and will therefore be loved by him, he is very loyal and affectionate to his own people. He not only shares your house, he also shares your life, your joys and

Temperament in the English Cocker Spaniel is one of the first concerns of every breeder. Whether sold as a puppy for show, for the field or as a companion only, an English Cocker must be sweet and reliable.

your sorrows, and he has a special antenna for your moods. The bond between you and your English Cocker can become incredibly strong to the point that no words are needed.

Note that another quality of the English Cocker that receives special mention in the standard is his sporting, sturdy, active and lively nature. You must be prepared to give your English Cocker, when he has matured, at least an hour of free exercise every day. He will enjoy a walk through the park on lead, or even a shopping expedition, but he needs more. He needs to have the opportunity to stretch his legs, run at full speed and be able to pick up exciting smells that appeal to his gundog instinct. Provided that your dog comes reliably to you when called, that he stays within calling distance and that you choose safe areas for his free exercise, he will enjoy exploring woods, fields, dunes; he loves it all...and especially water. If the idea of a soaking wet and rather muddy dog does not appeal to you, you have to teach him right from the start to stay away from the water. Do not think that will be easy! A walk without a swim is, in the eyes of an English Cocker, only half a walk—and if there's nowhere to swim, a deep muddy puddle may suit him just fine!

His energy is endless. He will walk the same distance as you two or three times over, at full speed, without resting, and it only takes the ten minutes' drive home from the park to restore him. Once home, he's ready for you to play with him, throw a ball for him to fetch or whatever it takes to get rid of his energy.

Although the English Cocker is a smaller member of the Sporting Group, he has plenty of stamina and vigor. He was designed to work in the field and must do so tirelessly.

PHYSICAL CHARACTERISTICS

The English Cocker is a relatively small, compact dog, with a height of between 15 and 17 inches and an average weight of around 30 pounds. His small body, however, is big on strength and power—two characteristics that are very important for a dog whose main function is to work in the field. For the pet, rather than the working, English Cocker, this strength is evident in his boundless energy. This is a breed that never seems to tire, so be prepared to spend time participating in some type of physical activity with your English Cocker. Not only will he appreciate the outlet for his energy, he also will appreciate the time spent with you!

One of the most obvious and most striking physical characteristics of the breed is the coat. The coat is long, flat and silky, consisting of a top coat and an undercoat. The English Cocker's dense coat does require attention in grooming, both to keep it looking in top condition and to prevent any odor. Perhaps the most interesting feature of the English Cocker's coat is the wide variation of colors and color patterns that are seen. Even more interesting is that there can be personality differences within the breed based on coat color! More detail about this aspect of the English Cocker Spaniel is worth mentioning.

COAT COLOR AND VARIATIONS

Dr. Caius mentioned in his *Treatise of Englishe Dogges* the Aquaticus or Spaniell, who finds game in the water and who is either red-and-white, solid black or solid red. Later, in 1803, in the book *The Sportsman's Cabinet,* springing spaniels and cocking spaniels are mentioned in the colors black-and-white, liver-and-white, red-and-white and a recent color, seen on a dog imported from France, marble blue. Nowadays English Cocker Spaniels occur in no fewer than 17 different colors to be divided into two groups: the solids and the parti-colors.

There is sable-and-white in American Cockers, but so far I haven't seen this color on an English Cocker Spaniel. The standard is not very explicit on colors; it just says "various" and that in solids only a small white patch on the throat is allowed; solid colors are defined as black, liver and red. Tan markings on certain colors are also mentioned.

Before the war it was common practice to breed all of the colors together, but after the war the breeding was mainly solid to solid and parti-color to parti-color. In solids black is the dominant color, with red and black-and-tan being recessive. In other words, if a dominant black (black not carrying the gene for red) is mated to a dominant black, all of the puppies will be black. If the dominant black is mated to a black carrying the gene for red, all of the puppies will also be black, but some of them will be carrying the gene for red. If two blacks both carrying the gene for red are mated, theoretically 25% of the puppies will be dominant black, 50% will be black but will carry the gene for red and 25% will be red (Fig. 1). If a red is mated to a black with the gene for red, 50% will be red and 50% will be black (Fig. 2). Two reds mated together can only produce red.

To produce liver, both parents should—apart from the gene for liver—also have the gene for black. If two dogs with the gene for liver but without the gene for black were to be mated, the resulting puppies would all be red with brown pigmentation (instead of black). A liver dog with the

Expected Colors in Pure-bred English Cocker Spaniels

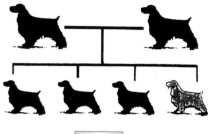

Fig. 1

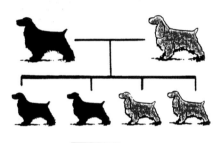

Fig. 2

Fig. 3

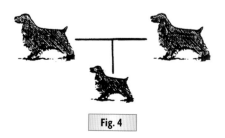

Fig. 4

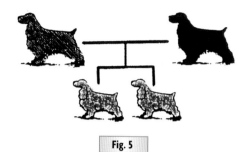

Fig. 5

Fig. 6

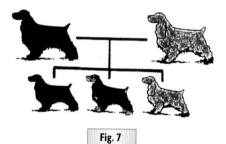

Fig. 7

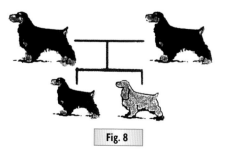

Fig. 8

genes for liver and for black mated to a black or a red without the gene for liver will only produce black puppies (Fig. 3). Liver pups can only be the result of a liver to liver or liver to brown-pigmented red combination (Fig. 4). A liver dog with the gene for red mated to a red or a black with the gene for red will produce red puppies (Fig. 5). A liver mated to a black-pigmented red (without the gene for liver) gives 25% to 50% black pups. This is the only way to breed black puppies out of non-black parents (Fig. 6).

Black-and-tans and liver-and-tans are in fact solids with recessive genes for tan. Solid is dominant and the tan pattern is recessive. The tan markings are genetically fixed, but the quantity of tan can differ greatly, as can the shade of tan. The only way to see whether a dog possesses the gene for tan is by breeding. A black and a red may both have the gene for tan and produce blacks, reds and black-and-tans (Fig. 7). Two black-and-tans produce 75% black-and-tan puppies. Should both of them have the gene for red, then 25% of the pups would be red-and-tan, but in practice this is invisible (Fig. 8). However, if such dogs were to be mated to black-and-tans without the gene for red, the offspring would be 100% black-and-tan (Fig. 9).

In parti-colors, blue roan is dominant over all other parti-

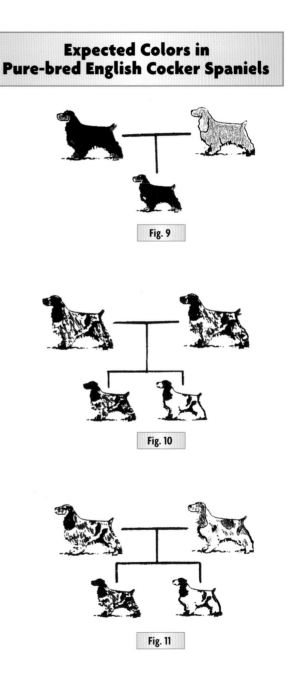

Expected Colors in Pure-bred English Cocker Spaniels

Fig. 9

Fig. 10

Fig. 11

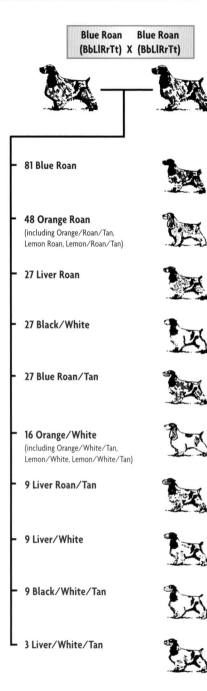

Blue Roan   Blue Roan
(BbLlRrTt) X (BbLlRrTt)

81 Blue Roan

48 Orange Roan
(including Orange/Roan/Tan,
Lemon Roan, Lemon/Roan/Tan)

27 Liver Roan

27 Black/White

27 Blue Roan/Tan

16 Orange/White
(including Orange/White/Tan,
Lemon/White, Lemon/White/Tan)

9 Liver Roan/Tan

9 Liver/White

9 Black/White/Tan

3 Liver/White/Tan

colors. Roan is dominant over ticking, but ticking is dominant over black-and-white or orange-and-white. Dark blue roan is dominant over light blue roan, which explains why we see so many more dark blue roans than black-and-whites or light blues. I bred three litters with a black-and-white bitch out of a black-and-white mother. All three sires were blue (with black-and-whites in their pedigrees) and out of all three litters I had only one black-and-white. To have black-and-white puppies out of her, I would have had to mate her to a black-and-white or orange-and-white dog (Fig. 10).

A black-and-white is, in fact, a black dog with two genes for parti-color. Should he have one gene for roan and one for open-marked white, he himself would be a roan. A black-and-tan with two genes for parti-color becomes a tri-color or blue-roan-and-tan. If we breed an orange roan bitch to a black-and-white dog, their puppies will nearly all be dark blue roan.

In a newborn litter of parti-colors all of the puppies are black-and-white (or orange-and-white). The only way to see whether the puppy will later become a blue roan is by looking at his pads and nails. Should these be black right from the start, then you know that your puppy will be a blue roan. If they are pink, then the puppy will become a black-and-white. To produce tricolor puppies, both parents should have the gene for tan. The tan is only there where the markings are. Should you have a puppy with an irregular marking (i.e., one black eye/ear and one white eye/ear) the tan will only be found on the side where the black marking is. This is not a fault according to the standard, but most breeders do not like it.

We once mated a blue-roan-and-tan to an orange roan and the resulting puppies were all blue roan or black-and-white. Conclusion? The blue-roan-and-tan missed the gene for orange and the orange roan missed the gene for tan (Fig. 11). Although the puppies were blue, they all carried the gene for tan and for orange. Should we mate such a blue with these two genes to a liver roan, what will happen then? Chances are the whole litter is blue roan, but it might just be possible that you will have a "rainbow" litter with every color that's possible!

In parti-colors, the blue roan is dominant. This is a unique and attractive color pattern, as seen on these blue roan siblings.

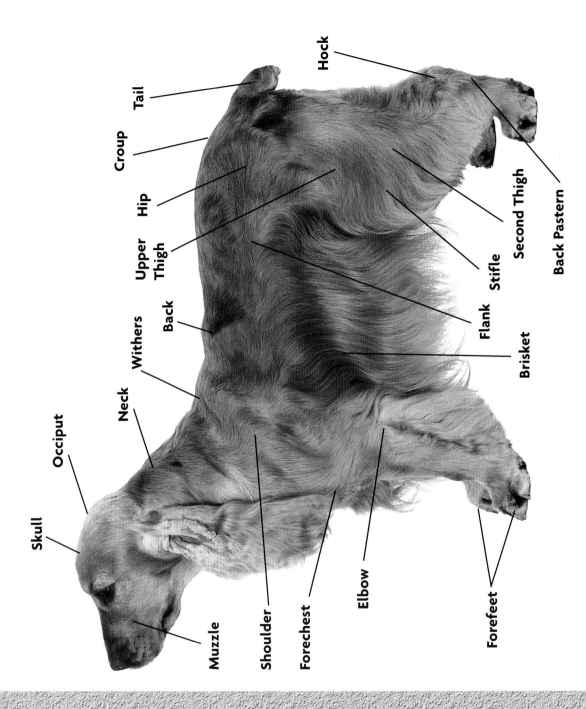

Hock

Tail

Croup

Hip

Upper
Thigh

Second Thigh

Back Pastern

Stifle

Withers

Back

Flank

Neck

Brisket

Occiput

Skull

Muzzle

Shoulder

Forechest

Elbow

Forefeet

PHYSICAL STRUCTURE OF THE ENGLISH COCKER SPANIEL

ENGLISH COCKER SPANIEL

The first breed standard for the English Cocker was written and officially approved by The Kennel Club in Great Britain in 1902. In later years some minor changes were made but, on the whole, the standard has remained practically unaltered. The British standard is also recognized by all FCI (Fédération Cynologique Internationale) member countries and its associates, which include most of continental Europe; a number of countries in South America, Asia and India; Australia and New Zealand; and more. The American Kennel Club standard, presented here, is slightly different, certainly more extensive and with a slight difference in the ideal size and weight.

How exciting to wear the ribbons of a winner! This is a lovely and successful English Cocker.

THE AMERICAN KENNEL CLUB BREED STANDARD FOR THE ENGLISH COCKER SPANIEL

General Appearance: The English Cocker Spaniel is an active, merry sporting dog, standing well up at the withers and compactly built. He is alive with energy; his gait is powerful and frictionless, capable both of covering ground effortlessly and penetrating dense cover to flush and retrieve game. His enthusiasm in the field and the incessant action of his tail while at work indicate how much he enjoys the hunting for which he was bred. His head is especially characteristic. He is, above all, a dog of balance, both standing and moving, without exaggeration in any part, the whole worth more than the sum of its parts.

Size, Proportion, Substance:
Size—Height at withers: males, 16 to 17 inches; females, 15 to 16 inches. Deviations to be penalized. The most desirable weights: males, 28 to 34 pounds; females, 26 to 32 pounds. Proper conformation and substance should be considered more important than weight alone. *Proportion*—Compactly built and short-coupled, with height at withers slightly greater than the distance from withers to set-on of tail. *Substance*—The English Cocker is a solidly built dog with as much bone and substance as is possible without becoming cloddy or coarse.

Head: General appearance: strong, yet free from coarseness, softly contoured, without sharp angles.

This English Cocker exhibits many positive qualities according to the standard. Notice the graceful neck, long silky hair on the ears and compact body, to name a few desirable traits.

Taken as a whole, the parts combine to produce the expression distinctive of the breed. *Expression*—Soft, melting, yet dignified, alert and intelligent. *Eyes*—The eyes are essential to the desired expression. They are medium in size, full and slightly oval; set wide apart; lids tight. Haws are inconspicuous; may be pigmented or unpigmented. Eye color dark brown, except in livers and liver parti-colors where hazel is permitted, but the darker the hazel the better. *Ears*—Set low, lying close to the head; leather fine, extending to the nose, well covered with long, silky, straight or slightly wavy hair. *Skull*—Arched and slightly flattened when seen both from the side and from the front. Viewed in profile, the brow appears not appreciably higher than the back-skull. Viewed from above, the sides of the skull are in planes roughly parallel to those of the muzzle. Stop definite, but moderate, and slightly grooved. *Muzzle*—Equal in length to skull; well cushioned; only as much narrower than the skull as is consistent with a full eye placement; cleanly chiseled under the eyes. Jaws strong, capable of carrying game. Nostrils wide for proper development of scenting ability; color black, except in livers and parti-colors of that shade where they will be brown; reds and parti-colors of that shade may be brown, but black is preferred. Lips square, but not pendulous or showing prominent flews. *Bite*—Scissors. A level bite is not preferred. Overshot or undershot to be severely penalized.

Neck, Topline and Body: *Neck*— Graceful and muscular, arched toward the head and blending cleanly, without throatiness, into sloping shoulders; moderate in length and in balance with the length and height of the dog. *Topline*—The line of the neck blends into the shoulder and backline in a smooth curve. The backline slopes very slightly toward a gently rounded croup, and is free from sagging or rumpiness. *Body*—Compact and well-knit, giving the impression of strength without heaviness. Chest deep; not so wide as to interfere with action of forelegs, nor so narrow as to allow the front to appear narrow or pinched. Forechest well developed, prosternum projecting moderately beyond shoulder points. Brisket reaches to the elbow and slopes gradually to a moderate tuck-up. Ribs well sprung and springing gradually to mid-body, tapering to back ribs which are of good depth and extend well back. Back short and strong. Loin short, broad and very slightly arched, but not enough to affect the topline appreciably. Croup gently rounded, without any tendency to

One of the many charms of the English Cocker Spaniel is the wide range of colors in which the breed occurs.

fall away sharply. *Tail*—Docked. Set on to conform to croup. Ideally, the tail is carried horizontally and is in constant motion while the dog is in action. Under excitement, the dog may carry his tail somewhat higher, but not cocked up.

Forequarters: The English Cocker is moderately angulated. Shoulders are sloping, the blade flat and smoothly fitting. Shoulder blade and upper arm are approximately equal in length. Upper arm set well back, joining the shoulder with sufficient angulation to place the elbow beneath the highest point of the shoulder blade when the dog is standing naturally. *Forelegs*—Straight, with bone nearly uniform in size from elbow to heel; elbows set close to the

EARS

Set low; hair is long, straight and silky (left). Ears on the right are too short.

HEAD

Should have moderately pronounced occiput (left). Skull on the right is too round.

SKULL

Two examples of an incorrect head: Skull shorter than muzzle (left) and skull longer than muzzle (right).

FEET

Should have straight, firm pasterns and round, thickly padded feet (left). On the right, the pastern is overly angulated and the foot is elongated.

TAIL

Should be carried level (left), never cocked up (right).

body; pasterns nearly straight, with some flexibility. *Feet*—Proportionate in size to the legs, firm, round and catlike; toes arched and tight; pads thick.

Hindquarters: Angulation moderate and, most importantly, in balance with that of the forequarters. Hips relatively broad and well rounded. Upper thighs broad, thick and muscular, providing plenty of propelling power. Second thighs well muscled and approximately equal in length to the upper. Stifle strong and well bent. Hock to pad short. Feet as in front.

Coat: On head, short and fine; of medium length on body; flat or slightly wavy; silky in texture. The English Cocker is well-feathered, but not so profusely as to interfere with field work. Trimming is permitted to remove overabundant hair and to enhance the dog's true lines. It should be done so as to appear as natural as possible.

Color: Various. Parti-colors are either clearly marked, ticked or roaned, the white appearing in combination with black, liver or shades of red. In parti-colors it is preferable that solid markings be broken on the body and more or less evenly distributed; absence of body markings is acceptable. Solid colors are black, liver or shades of red. White feet on a solid are undesirable; a little white on throat is acceptable; but in neither case do these white markings make the dog a parti-color. Tan markings, clearly defined and of rich shade, may appear in conjunction with black, livers and parti-color combinations of those colors. Black and tans and liver and tans are considered solid colors.

Gait: The English Cocker is capable of hunting in dense cover and upland terrain. His gait is accordingly characterized more by drive and the appearance of power than by great speed. He covers ground effortlessly and with extension both in front and in rear, appropriate to his angulation. In the ring, he carries his head proudly and is able to keep much the same topline while in action as when standing for examination. Going and coming, he moves in a straight line without crabbing or rolling, and with width between both front and rear legs appropriate to his build and gait.

Temperament: The English Cocker is merry and affectionate, of equable disposition, neither sluggish nor hyperactive, a willing worker and a faithful and engaging companion.

Approved October 11, 1988
Effective November 30, 1988

If an English Cocker Spaniel doesn't capture your heart (hard to believe!), adding a puppy to the equation surely will. A pup will learn many valuable lessons in the time spent with his dam.

ENGLISH COCKER SPANIEL

CHOOSING YOUR PUPPY

You've decided that you want to share your life with an English Cocker Spaniel. This is the breed that you feel suits you best in temperament and in lifestyle. What do you plan to do with your new puppy? Do you want to get moving with your English Cocker by joining agility classes? Would you like to do obedience training or are you interested in being able to take a dog on a shoot? Your choice of an English Cocker Spaniel means that you will be able to do all of these things if

Selecting the puppy best suited for your lifestyle is not easy. It's hard to resist the English Cocker's sweet expression, but you must use your head as well as your heart.

you choose. By deciding on the English Cocker Spaniel, you have chosen a companion with a very happy temperament, who thinks life is wonderful and who will love you indiscriminately.

Now, before you go to a breeder, there are a few questions that need to be answered. Do you have a color preference? There are a few considerations. A red one will usually have an easy coat that does not require too much trimming. Some blacks have natural non-trim coats, but the majority grow a lot of hair and have to be trimmed every six to eight weeks. The same goes for the parti-colors: oranges usually do not have much surplus hair

NEW RELEASES

Most breeders release their puppies between eight and ten weeks of age. A breeder who allows puppies to leave the litter at five or six weeks of age may be more concerned with profit than with the puppies' welfare. However, some breeders of show or working breeds may hold one or more top-quality puppies longer, occasionally until four months of age or even older, in order to evaluate the puppies' career or show potential and decide which one(s) they will keep for themselves.

SIGNS OF A HEALTHY PUPPY

Healthy puppies are robust little fellows who are alert and active, sporting shiny coats and supple skin. They should not appear lethargic, bloated or pot-bellied, nor should they have flaky skin or runny or crusted eyes or noses. Their stools should be firm and well formed, with no evidence of blood or mucus.

and only need occasional trimming of the head, ears, feet and tail, but blue roans have a heavier coat and will have to be trimmed every six to eight weeks.

Color is just one consideration. Will your English Cocker Spaniel be a dog or a bitch? It is often said that a bitch is sweeter than a dog, but in my experience the dogs are just as sweet as the bitches and are also very easygoing.

Will he be simply a much-loved pet or would you like to show your English Cocker in the future? It is very important that you explain all of your preferences to the breeder so that he can help you pick the puppy that is best suited to you and that shows good potential for your future pursuits.

There is a very general difference in temperaments related to coat color. The solids are highly intelligent and therefore need a firm hand. The personalities of the puppies in a litter also may differ slightly. Explain to the breeder what you prefer: the softer, sweeter one or the outgoing, cheeky puppy.

If you have the time and dedication to train your puppy and treat him consistently and fairly at all times, there is no better pet than an English Cocker Spaniel.

English Cockers of correct temperament will rush to greet new people and will welcome attention and human handling.

Observe the pups with their dam. Seeing the mother will give you some idea of the eventual color, size and temperament of the pups in the litter.

FINDING A BREEDER

Before getting in touch with a breeder, it may help you to visit a couple of all-breed dog shows where the English Cocker is competing or even a breed specialty show, which means that only English Cockers will be competing. Watch the handlers and how they communicate with their dogs, observe all of the dogs and see which breeder has dogs with the type and temperament you like. You also should contact the national breed club, the English Cocker Spaniel Club of America, and ask for referrals to member breeders in your region. The club will give you a list of breeders who adhere to the club's rules and code of ethics. These rules mainly concern responsible breeding, good conduct and overall betterment of the breed. The club also has a rescue program to rehome adult English Cockers.

GETTING ACQUAINTED

When visiting a litter, ask the breeder for suggestions on how best to interact with the puppies. If possible, get right into the middle of the pack and sit down with them. Observe which pups climb into your lap and which ones shy away. Toss a toy for them to chase and bring back to you. It's easy to fall in love with the puppy who picks you, but keep your future objectives in mind before you make your final decision.

A SHOW PUPPY

If you plan to show your puppy, you must first deal with a reputable breeder who shows his dogs and has had some success in the conformation ring. The puppy's pedigree should include one or more champions in the first and second generation. You should be familiar with the breed and breed standard so you can know what qualities to look for in your puppy. The breeder's observations and recommendations also are invaluable aids in selecting your future champion. If you consider an older puppy, be sure that the puppy has been properly socialized with people and not isolated in a kennel without substantial daily human contact.

If you visit a breeder and you are a bit doubtful about the puppies, the breeder or the conditions in which the puppies are kept, or if the breeder thinks that testing for hereditary defects is not necessary, do not buy! You must be 100% sure; buying because you are afraid to say no or because you feel sorry for the pup is wrong. After all, you are going to buy a companion who will be part of your family for the next 12 to 14 years and you must be absolutely certain about your decision.

Should you want to buy a puppy for showing, discuss this with the breeder. Also discuss with him what to do in case the puppy ends up as being not suitable for showing. Unforeseen

A good way to find an English Cocker breeder is to visit a dog show and look for dogs that strike your fancy. You then can meet at the show or find out how to contact the breeder(s) of these dogs.

changes may happen as the pup grows, and if you are very determined to have a show-quality pup you might do better to buy a more mature puppy, say six to seven months old, at which age it will be evident if the pup is or is not a show prospect.

Whether you are buying an English Cocker Spaniel pup for pet or for show, it is equally important to find out about the pup's medical background. Inquire about inoculations and when the puppy was last dosed for worms. Even more importantly, ask to see documentation that the parents of the litter have had appropriate testing done for hereditary defects. Your breeder should openly discuss genetic problems in the breed and his line.

It is nowadays common practice to sell a puppy with a

THE FAMILY TREE

Your puppy's pedigree is his family tree. Just as a child may resemble his parents and grandparents, so too will a puppy reflect the qualities, good and bad, of his ancestors, especially those in the first two generations. Therefore it's important to know as much as possible about a puppy's immediate relatives. Reputable and experienced breeders should be able to explain the pedigree and why they chose to breed from the particular dogs they used.

Raising a litter of English Cockers is time-consuming, food-consuming and money-consuming. Good breeders rarely make a profit on puppy sales. For true breeders, a litter is a labor of love and the pursuit of excellence in their breed.

PEDIGREE VS. REGISTRATION CERTIFICATE

Too often new owners are confused between these two important documents. Your puppy's pedigree, essentially a family tree, is a written record of a dog's genealogy of three generations or more. The pedigree will show you the names as well as performance titles of all dogs in your pup's background. Your breeder must provide you with a registration application, with his part properly filled out. You must complete the application and send it to the AKC with the proper fee. Every puppy must come from a litter that has been AKC-registered by the breeder, born in the US and from a sire and dam that are also registered with the AKC.

The seller must provide you with complete records to identify the puppy. The AKC requires that the seller provide the buyer with the following: breed; sex, color and markings; date of birth; litter number (when available); names and registration numbers of the parents; breeder's name; and date sold or delivered.

sales contract. This is fine, but do not sign on the spot. Ask the breeder if you can take it home before purchasing the pup to read it carefully so that you know exactly what you are going to sign. More important than a sales contract, however, is a good relationship between you and the breeder. A responsible, dedicated breeder is at all times willing to answer all your questions, to calm your fears and to share your joys.

BUYING YOUR PUPPY
You have contacted a breeder, he has a litter and there you are, surrounded by all of these lovely puppies. How will you ever be able to choose? For instance, if you have decided that you want a bitch puppy, ask the breeder to take the male puppies away to make the choice a bit easier. Now what you are looking for is a healthy, good-looking, happy little thing that will be all over you in no time when you crouch down, thinking you are great fun. Do not go for a shy pup, but do not go for a bully either. Ask the breeder

if you can see the dam (and sire if possible) and see what her temperament is like. Discuss the pedigrees of both parents with him so that you can make sure that your puppy comes from good stock.

All of this may seem like a lot of effort…and you have not even brought the pup home yet! Breed research, breeder selection and puppy visitation are very important aspects of finding the puppy of your dreams. Beyond that, these things also lay the foundation for a successful future with your pup. We've discussed how puppy personalities within each litter vary, from the shy and easygoing puppy to the one who is dominant and assertive, with most pups falling somewhere in between. By spending time with the puppies, you will be able to recognize certain behaviors and what these behaviors indicate about each pup's temperament. Which type of pup will complement your family dynamics is best

FINDING A QUALIFIED BREEDER

Before you begin your puppy search, ask for references from your veterinarian, other breeders and other English Cocker owners to refer you to someone they believe is reputable. Responsible breeders usually raise only one or two breeds of dog. Avoid any breeder who has several different breeds or has several litters at the same time. Dedicated breeders are usually involved with a breed or other dog club. Many participate in some sport or activity related to their breed. Just as you want to be assured of the breeder's qualifications, the breeder wants to be assured that you will make a worthy owner. Expect the breeder to interview you, asking questions about your goals for the pup, your experience with dogs and what kind of home you will provide.

determined by observing the puppies in action within their "pack." Your breeder's expertise and recommendations are very

Watching the litter interact together is as fun as it is educational.

This English Cocker puppy is only a few days old. The eyes are closed for about the first week.

valuable. Although you may fall in love with a bold and brassy male, the breeder may suggest that another pup would be best for you. The breeder's experience in rearing English Cocker Spaniel pups and matching their temperaments with appropriate humans offer the best assurance that your pup will meet your needs and expectations. The type of puppy that you select is just as important as your decision that the English Cocker Spaniel is the breed for you.

The decision to live with an English Cocker Spaniel is a serious commitment and not one to be taken lightly. This puppy is

a living sentient being that will be dependent on you for basic survival for his entire life. Beyond the basics of survival—food, water, shelter and protection—he needs much, much more. The new pup needs love, nurturing and a proper canine education to mold him into a responsible, well-behaved canine citizen. Your English Cocker Spaniel's health and good manners will need consistent monitoring and regular "tune-ups," so your job as a responsible dog owner will be ongoing throughout every stage of his life. If you are not prepared to accept these responsibilities and commit to them for at least the next decade, very likely longer, then you are not prepared to own a dog of any breed.

Although the responsibilities of owning a dog may at times tax your patience, the joy of living with your English Cocker Spaniel far outweighs the workload, and a well-mannered adult dog is worth your time and effort. Before your

How happy you will be to hold and cuddle your new puppy! The puppy is probably just as happy as you are.

very eyes, your new charge will grow up to be your most loyal friend, devoted to you unconditionally.

YOUR ENGLISH COCKER SPANIEL SHOPPING LIST

Just as expectant parents prepare a nursery for their baby, so should you ready your home for the arrival of your English Cocker Spaniel pup. If you have the necessary puppy supplies purchased and in place before he comes home, it will ease the puppy's transition from the warmth and familiarity of his mom and littermates to the brand-new environment of his new home and human family. You will be too busy to stock up and prepare your house after your pup comes home, that's for sure! Imagine how a pup must feel upon being transported to a strange new place. It's up to you to comfort him and to let your little pup know that he is going to be happy with you.

COST OF OWNERSHIP
The purchase price of your puppy is merely the first expense in the typical dog budget. Quality dog food, veterinary care (sickness and health maintenance), dog supplies and grooming costs will add up to big bucks every year. Can you adequately afford to support a canine addition to the family?

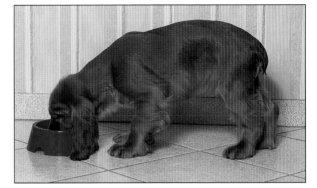

FOOD AND WATER BOWLS
Your puppy will need separate bowls for his food and water. Stainless steel pans are generally preferred over plastic bowls since they sterilize better and pups are less inclined to chew on the metal. Heavy-duty ceramic bowls are popular, but consider how often you will have to pick up those heavy bowls. Buy adult-sized bowls, as your English Cocker puppy will grow into them before you know it.

Pet shops sell special food and water bowls designed to keep the dog's ears out of the bowl when he is eating or drinking. These bowls are ideal for dogs like English Cockers that have long ears.

THE DOG CRATE
If you think that crates are tools of punishment and confinement for when a dog has misbehaved, think again. Most breeders and almost all trainers recommend a crate as the preferred house-training aid as well as for all-around puppy training and safety. Because dogs are natural den creatures that prefer cave-like environments, the benefits of crate use are many. The crate provides the puppy with his very own

The most common crate types: mesh on the left, wire on the right and fiberglass on top.

"safe house," a cozy place to sleep, take a break or seek comfort with a favorite toy; a travel aid to house your dog when on the road, at motels or at the vet's office; a training aid to help teach your puppy proper toileting habits; a place of solitude when non-dog people happen to drop by and don't want a lively puppy—or even a well-behaved adult dog—saying hello or begging for attention.

Crates come in several types, although the wire crate and the fiberglass airline-type crate are the most popular. Both are safe and your puppy will adjust to either one, so the choice is up to you. The wire crates offer better visibility for the pup as well as better ventilation. Many of the wire crates easily fold down into suitcase-size carriers. The fiberglass crates, similar to those used by the airlines for animal transport, are sturdier and more den-like. However, the fiberglass crates do not fold down and are less ventilated than a wire crate, which can be problematic in hot weather. Some of the newer crates are made of heavy plastic mesh; they are very lightweight and fold up into slim-line suitcases. However, a mesh crate might not be suitable for a pup with manic chewing habits.

Don't bother with a puppy-sized crate. Although your English Cocker Spaniel will be a wee fellow when you bring him home, he will grow up in the blink of an eye and your puppy crate will be useless. Purchase a crate that will accommodate an adult English Cocker Spaniel. He will stand up to 17 inches at the shoulder when full grown, so a crate of about 30

inches long by 21 inches wide by 24 inches high should fit him nicely. For the puppy, the crate can be partitioned with a removable panel to give him a smaller area. This helps with house-training and also helps pup to feel cozy rather than lost in a too-big crate.

BEDDING AND CRATE PADS
Your puppy will enjoy some type of soft bedding in his "room" (the crate), something he can snuggle into to feel cozy and secure. Old towels or blankets are good choices for a young pup, since he may (and probably will) have a toileting accident or two in the crate or decide to chew on the bedding material. Once he is fully trained and out of the early chewing stage, you can replace the puppy bedding with a

CRATE EXPECTATIONS
To make the crate more inviting to your puppy, you can offer his first meal or two inside the crate, always keeping the crate door open so that he does not feel confined. Keep a favorite toy or two in the crate for him to play with while inside. You can also cover the crate at night with a lightweight sheet to make it more den-like and remove the stimuli of household activity. Never put him into his crate as punishment or as you are scolding him, since he will then associate his crate with negative situations and avoid going there.

permanent crate pad if you prefer. Crate pads and other dog beds run the gamut from inexpensive to high-end doggie-designer styles, but don't splurge on the good stuff until you are sure that your puppy is reliable and won't tear it up, chew it up or make a mess on it.

English Cockers love to snuggle up with their canine companions and human friends.

PUPPY TOYS
Just as infants and older children require objects to stimulate their minds and bodies, puppies need toys to entertain their curious brains, wiggly paws and achy teeth. A fun array of safe doggie

Be sure to purchase an array of safe, interesting toys to keep his teeth *and* mind occupied in an acceptable way.

toys will help satisfy your puppy's chewing instincts and distract him from gnawing on the leg of your antique chair or your new leather sofa. Most puppy toys are cute and look as if they would be a lot of fun, but not all are necessarily safe or good for your puppy, so use caution when you go puppy-toy shopping.

Although English Cocker Spaniels are not known to be voracious chewers like many other dogs, they still love to chew. The best "chewcifiers" are nylon and hard rubber bones, which are safe to gnaw on and come in sizes appropriate for all age groups and breeds. Be especially careful of natural bones, which can splinter or develop dangerous sharp edges; pups can easily swallow or choke on those bone splinters. Veterinarians often tell of surgical nightmares involving bits of splintered bone, because in addition to the danger of choking, the sharp pieces can damage the intestinal tract.

Similarly, rawhide chews, while a favorite of most dogs and puppies, can be equally dangerous. Pieces of rawhide are easily swallowed after they get soft and gummy from chewing, and dogs have been known to choke on pieces of ingested rawhide. Rawhide chews should be offered only when you can supervise the puppy (or adult).

CONFINEMENT

It is wise to keep your puppy confined to a small "puppy-proofed" area of the house for his first few weeks at home. Gate or block off a space near the door he will use for outdoor potty trips. Expandable baby gates are useful to create puppy's designated area. If he is allowed to roam through the entire house or even only several rooms, it will be more difficult to house-train him.

Soft woolly toys are special puppy favorites. They come in a wide variety of cute shapes and sizes; some look like little stuffed animals. Puppies love to shake them up and toss them about, or simply carry them around. Be careful of fuzzy toys that have button eyes or noses that your pup could chew off and swallow, and make sure that he does not disembowel a squeaky toy to remove the squeaker! Braided rope toys are similar in that they are fun to chew and toss around, but they shred easily and the strings are easy to swallow. The strings are not digestible and, if the puppy doesn't pass them in his stool, he could end up at the vet's office. As with rawhides, your puppy should be closely monitored with rope toys.

If you believe that your pup has ingested a piece of one of his toys, check his stools for the next couple of days to see if he passes the item when he defecates. At the same time, also watch for signs of intestinal distress. A call to your veterinarian might be in order to get his advice and be on the safe side.

An all-time favorite toy for puppies (young and old!) is the empty gallon milk jug. Hard plastic juice containers—46 ounces or more—are also excellent. Such containers make lots of noise when they are batted about, and puppies go crazy with

TOYS 'R SAFE
The vast array of tantalizing puppy toys is staggering. Stroll through any pet shop or pet-supply outlet and you will see that the choices can be overwhelming. However, not all dog toys are safe or sensible. Most very young puppies enjoy soft woolly toys that they can snuggle with and carry around. (You know they have outgrown them when they shred them up!) Avoid toys that have buttons, tabs or other enhancements that can be chewed off and swallowed. Soft toys that squeak are fun, but make sure your puppy does not disembowel the toy and remove (and swallow) the squeaker. Toys that rattle or make noise can excite a puppy, but they present the same danger as the squeaky kind and so require supervision. Hard rubber toys that bounce can also entertain a pup, but make sure that the toy is too big for your pup to swallow.

delight as they play with them. However, they don't often last very long, so be sure to remove and replace them when they get chewed up.

A word of caution about homemade toys: be careful with your choices of non-traditional play objects. Never use old shoes or socks, since a puppy cannot distinguish between the old ones on which he's allowed to chew and the new ones in your closet that are strictly off limits. That principle applies to anything that resembles something that you don't want your puppy to chew.

COLLARS

A lightweight nylon collar is the best choice for a very young pup. Quick-clip collars are easy to put on and remove, and they can be adjusted as the puppy grows.

A lightweight nylon buckle collar is the best choice for your growing English Cocker puppy.

> **TEETHING TIME**
> All puppies chew. It's normal canine behavior. Chewing just plain feels good to a puppy, especially during the three- to five-month teething period when the adult teeth are breaking through the gums. Rather than attempting to eliminate such a strong natural chewing instinct, you will be more successful if you redirect it and teach your puppy what he may or may not chew. Correct inappropriate chewing with a sharp "No!" and offer him a chew toy, praising him when he takes it. Don't become discouraged. Chewing usually decreases after the adult teeth have come in.

Introduce him to his collar as soon as he comes home to get him accustomed to wearing it. He'll get used to it quickly and won't mind a bit. Make sure that it is snug enough that it won't slip off, yet loose enough to be comfortable for the pup. You should be able to slip two fingers between the collar and his neck. Check the collar often, as puppies grow in spurts, and his collar can become too tight almost overnight. Training collars should not be used on young puppies; the buckle collar will suffice.

LEASHES

A 6-foot nylon lead is an excellent choice for a young puppy. It is lightweight and not as tempting to chew as a leather lead. You can

This adorable orange roan puppy can't hide the fact that he's been getting into something!

switch to a 6-foot leather lead after your pup has grown and is used to walking politely on a lead. For initial puppy walks and house-training purposes, you should invest in a shorter lead so that you have more control over the puppy. At first, you don't want him wandering too far away from you, and when taking him out for toileting you will want to keep him in the specific area chosen for his potty spot.

Once the puppy is heel-trained with a traditional leash, you can consider purchasing a retractable lead. A retractable lead is excellent for walking adult dogs that are already leash-wise. This type of lead lengthens to allow the dog to roam farther away from you and explore a wider area when out walking, and also retracts when you need to keep him close to you.

HOME SAFETY FOR YOUR ENGLISH COCKER PUPPY

The importance of puppy-proofing cannot be overstated. In addition to making your house comfortable for your English Cocker Spaniel's arrival, you also must make sure that your house is safe for your puppy before you bring him home. There are countless hazards in the owner's personal living environment that a pup can sniff, chew, swallow or destroy. Many are obvious; others are not. Do a thorough advance house check to remove or rearrange those things that could hurt your puppy, keeping any potentially dangerous items out of areas to which he will have access.

CREATE A SCHEDULE

Puppies thrive on sameness and routine. Offer meals at the same time each day, take him out at regular times for potty trips and do the same for play periods and outdoor activity. Make note of when your puppy naps and when he is most lively and energetic, and try to plan his day around those times. Once he is house-trained and more predictable in his habits, he will be better able to tolerate changes in his schedule.

Electrical cords are especially dangerous, since puppies view them as irresistible chew toys. Unplug and remove all exposed cords or fasten them beneath baseboards where the puppy cannot reach them. Veterinarians and firefighters can tell you horror stories about electrical burns and house fires that resulted from puppy-chewed electrical cords. Consider this a most serious precaution for your puppy and the rest of your family.

Scout your home for tiny objects that might be seen at a pup's eye level. Keep medication bottles and cleaning supplies well

KEEP OUT OF REACH

Most dogs don't browse around your medicine cabinet, but accidents do happen! The drug acetaminophen, the active ingredient in some popular over-the-counter pain relievers, can be deadly to dogs and cats if ingested in large quantities. Acetaminophen toxicity, caused by the dog's swallowing 15 to 20 tablets, can be manifested in abdominal pains within a day or two of ingestion, as well as liver damage. If you suspect your dog has swiped a bottle of medicine, get the dog to the vet immediately so that the vet can induce vomiting and cleanse the dog's stomach.

A week-old puppy whose eyes are just starting to open.

out of reach, and do the same with waste baskets and other trash containers. It goes without saying that you should not use rodent poison or other toxic chemicals in any puppy area and that you must keep such containers safely locked up. You will be amazed at how many places a curious puppy can discover!

Once your house has cleared inspection, check your yard. A sturdy fence, well embedded into the ground, will give your dog a safe place to play and potty. Although English Cocker Spaniels are not known to be climbers or fence jumpers, they are still athletic dogs, so a 6-foot-high fence should be adequate to

A Dog-Safe Home

The dog-safety police are taking you on a house tour. Let's go room by room and see how safe your own home is for your new English Cocker. The following items are doggie dangers, so either they must be removed or the dog should be monitored or not allowed access to these areas.

Outdoors
- swimming pool
- pesticides
- toxic plants
- lawn fertilizers, mulch

Living Room
- house plants (some varieties are poisonous)
- fireplace or wood-burning stove
- paint on the walls (lead-based paint is toxic)
- lead drapery weights (toxic lead)
- lamps and electrical cords
- carpet cleaners or deodorizers

Bathroom
- blue water in the toilet bowl
- medicine cabinet (filled with potentially deadly bottles)
- soap bars, bleach, drain cleaners, etc.
- tampons

Kitchen
- household cleaners in the kitchen cabinets
- glass jars and canisters
- sharp objects (like kitchen knives, scissors and forks)
- garbage can (with remnants of good-smelling things like onions, potato skins, apple or pear cores, peach pits, coffee beans and other harmful tidbits)
- food left out on counters (some foods are toxic to dogs)

Garage
- antifreeze
- fertilizers (including rose foods)
- pesticides and rodenticides
- pool supplies (chlorine and other chemicals)
- oil and gasoline in containers
- sharp objects, electrical cords and power tools

English Cocker puppies are very curious. Sniffing and chewing are how they investigate; be certain that there are no toxic plants, fertilizers or other dangerous items that your pup could ingest.

contain an agile youngster or adult. Check the fence periodically for necessary repairs. If there is a weak link or space to squeeze through, you can be sure that a determined English Cocker Spaniel will discover it.

The garage and shed can be hazardous places for a pup, as things like fertilizers, chemicals and tools are usually kept there. It's best to keep these areas off limits to the pup. Antifreeze is especially dangerous to dogs, as they find the taste appealing and it takes only a few licks from the driveway to kill a dog, puppy or adult, small breed or large.

A very alert blue roan and tan English Cocker Spaniel puppy. Don't let the angelic look fool you. This industrious little puppy can make quite a mess without proper supervision.

VISITING THE VETERINARIAN

A good veterinarian is your English Cocker Spaniel puppy's best health-insurance policy. If you do not already have a vet, ask friends and experienced dog people in your area for recommendations so that you can select a vet before you bring your English Cocker Spaniel puppy home. Also arrange for your puppy's first veterinary examination beforehand, since many vets do not have appointments available immediately and your puppy should visit the vet within a day or so of coming home.

It's important to make sure that puppy's first visit to the vet is a pleasant and positive one. The vet should take great care to befriend the pup and handle him gently to make their first meeting a positive experience. The vet will give the pup a thorough physical examination and set up a schedule for vaccinations and other necessary wellness visits. Be sure to show your vet any health and inoculation records, which you should have received from your breeder. Your vet is a great source of canine health information, so be sure to ask questions and take notes. Creating a health journal for your puppy will make a handy reference for his wellness and any future health problems that may arise.

MEETING THE FAMILY

Your English Cocker Spaniel's homecoming is an exciting time for all members of the family, and it's only natural that everyone will be eager to meet him, pet him and play with him. However, for the puppy's sake, it's best to make these initial family meetings as uneventful as possible so that the pup is not overwhelmed with too much too soon. Remember, he has just left his dam and his littermates and is away from the breeder's home for the first time. Despite his fuzzy wagging tail, he

is still apprehensive and wondering where he is and who all these strange humans are. It's best to let him explore on his own and meet the family members as he feels comfortable. Let him investigate all of the new smells, sights and sounds at his own pace. Children should be especially careful to not get overly excited, use loud voices or hug the pup too tightly. Be calm,

This pensive black English Cocker puppy has lots to soak up in his brand-new environment. Keep activities low-key until the puppy becomes acquainted with his new family and settles in.

gentle and affectionate, and be ready to comfort him if he appears frightened or uneasy.

Be sure to show your puppy his new crate during this first day home. Toss a treat or two inside the crate; if he associates the crate with food, he will associate the crate with good things. If he is comfortable with the crate, you can offer him his first meal inside it. Leave the door ajar so he can wander in and out as he chooses.

FIRST NIGHT IN HIS NEW HOME

So much has happened in your English Cocker Spaniel puppy's first day away from the breeder. He's had his first car ride to his new home. He's met his new human family and perhaps the other family pets. He has explored his new house and yard, at least those places where he is to be allowed during his first weeks at home. He may have visited his new veterinarian. He has eaten his

PUPPY PARASITES
Parasites are nasty little critters that live in or on your dog or puppy. Most puppies are born with ascarid roundworms, which are acquired from dormant ascarids residing in the dam. Other parasites can be acquired through contact with infected fecal matter. Take a stool sample to your vet for testing. He will prescribe a safe wormer to treat any parasites found in your puppy's stool. Always have a fecal test performed at your puppy's annual veterinary exam.

first meal or two away from his dam and littermates. Surely that's enough to tire out an eight-week-old English Cocker Spaniel pup...or so you hope!

It's bedtime. During the day, the pup investigated his crate, which is his new den and sleeping space, so it is not entirely strange to him. Line the crate with a soft towel or blanket that he can snuggle into and gently place him into the crate for the night. Some breeders send home a piece of bedding from where the pup slept with his littermates, and those familiar scents are a great comfort for the puppy on his first night without his siblings.

Puppies need rest. Even the most feisty of Cocker puppies will need to nap after a burst of activity.

He will probably whine or cry. The puppy is objecting to the confinement and the fact that he is alone for the first time. This can be a stressful time for you as well as for the pup. It's important that you remain strong and don't let the puppy out of his crate to comfort him. He will fall asleep eventually. If you release him, the puppy will learn that crying means "out" and will continue that habit. You are laying the groundwork for future habits. Some breeders find that soft music can soothe a crying pup and help him get to sleep.

SOCIALIZING YOUR PUPPY

The first 20 weeks of your English Cocker Spaniel puppy's life are the most important of his entire lifetime. A properly socialized puppy will grow up to be a confident and stable adult who will be a pleasure to live with and a welcome addition to the neighborhood.

The importance of socialization cannot be overemphasized. Research on canine behavior has proven that puppies who are not exposed to new sights, sounds, people and animals during their first 20 weeks of life will grow up to be timid and fearful, even aggressive, and unable to flourish outside of their familiar home environment.

Socializing your puppy is not difficult and, in fact, will be a fun

SELECTING FROM THE LITTER
Before you visit a litter of puppies, promise yourself that you won't fall for the first pretty face you see! Decide on your goals for your puppy—show prospect, hunting dog, obedience competitor, family companion—and then look for a puppy who displays the appropriate qualities. In most litters, there is an Alpha pup (the bossy puppy), and occasionally a shy fellow who is less confident, with the rest of the litter falling somewhere in the middle. "Middle-of-the-roaders" are safe bets for most families and novice competitors.

time for you both. Lead training goes hand in hand with socialization, so your puppy will be learning how to walk on a lead at the same time that he's meeting the neighborhood. Because the

English Cocker Spaniel is such a terrific breed, everyone will enjoy meeting "the new kid on the block." Take him for short walks, to the park and to other dog-friendly places where he will encounter new people, especially children. Puppies automatically recognize children as "little people" and are drawn to play with them. Just make sure that you supervise these meetings and that the children do not get too rough or encourage him to play too hard. An overzealous pup can often nip too hard, frightening the child and in turn making the puppy overly excited. A bad experience in puppyhood can impact a dog for life, so a pup that has a negative experience with a child may grow up to be shy or even aggressive around children.

When raised with kindness and love, your English Cocker puppy will grow up to become a trusted member of your family.

Take your puppy along on your daily errands. Puppies are natural "people magnets," and most people who see your pup will want to pet him. All of these encounters will help to mold him into a confident adult dog. Likewise, you will soon feel like a confident, responsible dog owner, rightly proud of your mannerly English Cocker Spaniel.

Be especially careful of your puppy's encounters and experiences during the eight-to-ten-week-old period, which is also called the "fear period." This is a serious imprinting period, and all contact during this time should be gentle and positive. A frightening or negative event could leave a permanent impression that could affect his future behavior if a similar situation arises.

Also make sure that your puppy has received his first and second rounds of vaccinations before you expose him to other dogs or bring him to places that other dogs may frequent. Avoid dog parks and other strange-dog areas until your vet assures you that your puppy is fully immunized and resistant to the diseases that can be passed between canines. Discuss safe socialization with your breeder, as some breeders recommend socializing the puppy even before he has received all of his inoculations, depending on the individual puppy's temperament.

A quality-bred English Cocker puppy shines through. These two pups obviously have much to share with the right new owners.

LEADER OF THE PUPPY'S PACK

Like other canines, your puppy needs an authority figure, someone he can look up to and regard as the leader of his "pack." His first pack leader was his dam, who taught him to be polite and not chew too hard on her ears or nip at her muzzle. He learned those same lessons from his litter-mates. If he played too rough, they cried in pain and stopped the game, which sent an important message to the rowdy puppy.

As puppies play together, they are also struggling to determine who will be the boss. Being pack animals, dogs need someone to be in charge. If a litter of puppies remained together beyond puppyhood, one of the pups would emerge as the strongest one, the one who calls the shots.

Once your puppy leaves the pack, he will look intuitively for a new leader. If he does not recognize you as that leader, he will try to assume that position for himself. Of course, it is hard to imagine your adorable English Cocker Spaniel puppy trying to be in charge when he is so small and seemingly helpless. You must remember that these are natural canine instincts. Do not cave in and allow your pup to get the upper "paw"!

Just as socialization is so important during these first 20 weeks, so too is your puppy's early education. He was born without any bad habits. He does not know what is good or bad behavior. If he does things like nipping and digging, it's because he is having fun and doesn't know that humans consider these things as "bad." It's your job to teach him proper puppy manners, and this is the best time to accomplish that...before he has developed bad habits, since it is much more difficult to "unlearn" or correct unacceptable learned behavior than to teach good behavior from the start.

Make sure that all members of the family understand the importance of being consistent when training their new puppy. If you tell the puppy to stay off the sofa and your daughter allows him to cuddle on the couch to watch her favorite television show, your pup will be confused about what he is and is not allowed to do. Have a family conference before your pup comes home so that everyone understands the basic principles of puppy training and the rules you have set forth for the pup, and agrees to follow them.

The old saying that "an ounce of prevention is worth a pound of cure" is especially true when it comes to puppies. It is much easier to prevent inappropriate behavior than it is to change it. It's also easier and less stressful for the pup, since it will keep discipline to a minimum and create a more positive learning environment for him. That, in turn, will also be easier on you.

SOLVING PUPPY PROBLEMS

Puppy Whining

Puppies often cry and whine, just as infants and little children do. It's their way of telling us that they are lonely or in need of attention. Your puppy will miss his littermates and will feel insecure when he is left alone. You may be out of the house or just in another room, but he will still feel alone. During these times, the puppy's crate should be his personal comfort station, a place all his own where he can feel safe and secure. Once he learns that being alone is okay and not something to be feared, he will settle down without crying or objecting. You might want to leave a radio on while he is crated, as the sound of human voices can be soothing and will give the impression that people are around.

Give your puppy a favorite cuddly toy or chew toy to

A seven-week-old black English Cocker puppy in an alert stance. Something has caught his attention.

Puppies are comforted by the constant companionship of their mom and littermates. They may whine because they miss their canine family when they go to new homes, but they will quickly adjust to their human "packs."

entertain him whenever he is crated. You will both be happier: the puppy because he is safe in his den and you because he is quiet, safe and not getting into puppy escapades that can wreak havoc in your house or cause him danger.

To make sure that your puppy will always view his crate as a safe and cozy place, never, ever, use the crate as punishment. That's the best way to turn the crate into a negative place that the pup will want to avoid. Sure, you can use the crate for your own peace of mind if your puppy is getting into trouble and needs some "time out." Just don't let him know that! Never scold the pup and immediately place him into the crate. Count to ten, give him a couple of hugs and maybe a treat, then scoot him into his crate.

It's also important not to make a big fuss when he is released from the crate. That will make getting out of the crate more appealing than being in the crate, which is just the opposite of what you are trying to achieve.

"Counter Surfing"

What we like to call "counter surfing" is very similiar to jumping and usually starts to happen as soon as a puppy realizes that he is big enough to stand on his hind legs and investigate the good stuff on the kitchen counter or the coffee table. Once again, you have to be there to prevent it! As soon as you see your English Cocker Spaniel even start to raise himself up, startle him with a sharp "No!" or "Aaahh, aaahh!" If he succeeds and manages to get one or both paws on the forbidden surface,

A look into an
English Cocker's
sweet face can
melt anyone's
heart.

tell him "Off!" as you lower him back to all fours on the ground. As soon as he's back on all four paws, command him to sit and praise at once.

For surf prevention, make sure to keep any tempting treats or edibles out of reach, where your English Cocker Spaniel can't see or smell them. It's the old rule of prevention yet again.

FOOD GUARDING

Some dogs are picky eaters; others seem to inhale their food without chewing it. Occasionally the true "chow hound" will become protective of his food, which is one dangerous step toward other aggressive behavior. Food guarding is obvious: your puppy will growl, snarl or even attempt to bite you if you approach his food bowl or put your hand into his pan while he's eating.

This behavior is not acceptable, and very preventable! If your puppy is an especially voracious eater, sit next to him occasionally while he eats and dangle your fingers in his food bowl. Don't feed him in a corner, where he could feel possessive of his eating space. Rather, place his food bowl in an open area of your kitchen where you are in close proximity. Occasionally remove his food in mid-meal, tell him he's a good boy and return his bowl.

If your pup becomes possessive of his food, look for other signs of future aggression, like guarding his favorite toys or refusing to obey obedience commands that he knows. Consult an obedience trainer for help in reinforcing obedience so your English Cocker Spaniel will fully understand that *you* are the boss.

REPEAT YOURSELF

Puppies learn best through repetition. Use the same verbal cues and commands when teaching your puppy new behaviors or correcting for misbehaviors. Be consistent, but not monotonous. Puppies get bored just like puppy owners.

PROPER CARE OF YOUR

ENGLISH COCKER SPANIEL

Adding an English Cocker Spaniel to your household means adding a new family member who will need your care each and every day. When your English Cocker Spaniel pup first comes home, you will start a routine with him so that, as he grows up, your dog will have a daily schedule just as you do. The aspects of your dog's daily care will likewise become regular parts of your day, so you'll both have a new schedule. Dogs learn by consistency and thrive on routine: regular times for meals, exercise, grooming and potty trips are just as important for your dog as they are to you! Your dog's schedule will depend much on your family's daily routine, but remember that you now have a new member of the family who is part of your day every day.

FEEDING
Feeding your dog the best diet is based on various factors, including age, activity level, overall condition and size of breed. When you visit the breeder, he will share with you his advice about the proper diet for your dog based on his experience with the breed and the foods with which he has had

success. Likewise, your vet will be a helpful source of advice throughout the dog's life and will aid you in planning a diet for optimal health.

There are four basic types of dog foods: fresh meat; dry food; semi-moist food and canned food. If offering fresh meat, many English Cocker owners find that their dogs love tripe. You can combine meat portions with dry food or with a semi-moist food. Dry foods are less expensive, more convenient and usually nutrition- ally balanced, but dogs may get bored with them. How would you

You are what you eat—and this goes for dogs too! Feed your dog a nutritionally complete food and make sure that whoever is responsible for the dog's food and water is reliable and consistent.

NOT HUNGRY?

No dog in his right mind would turn down his dinner, would he? If you notice that your dog has lost interest in his food, there could be any number of causes. Dental problems are a common cause of appetite loss, one that is often overlooked. If your dog has a toothache, a loose tooth or sore gums from infection, chances are it doesn't feel so good to chew. Think about when you've had a toothache! If your dog does not approach the food bowl with his usual enthusiasm, look inside his mouth for signs of a problem. Whatever the cause, you'll want to consult your vet so that your chow hound can get back to his happy, hungry self as soon as possible.

feel if you had the same meal day after day, year after year? It certainly doesn't do a dog any harm to surprise him with occasional healthy treats like a quarter of an apple, some carrots or lettuce.

PUPPY STAGE

When you decided to buy your puppy, the breeder probably told you what you should feed the puppy once you bring him home. If he didn't, ask him. This is important for two reasons; first, coming with you to live in totally new surroundings with so many new experiences is already a stressful experience for the puppy, and a continuation of his diet will help him adjust. Even then, his tummy may be upset the first couple of days, or he may even refuse to eat for a day or two, but don't worry about that. As soon as he is settled down he will eat again, especially if he's being fed the food he is used to. Second, the breeder most likely has a lot of experience in feeding mature dogs and puppies and keeping them in a peak condition, so it would be wise to listen to his advice. A good breeder will provide you with exact instructions of what to feed the puppy at each stage of his life and we strongly advise you to follow these instructions. Once your puppy is a mature one- or two-year-old, you can change his diet to what is more convenient for you (availability, costs, etc.), but with the growing puppy and youngster, stick to the breeder's diet. And remember that if ten breeders are discussing the feeding of their dogs, you will hear ten different opinions, and all of them will be right!

Your puppy will need three or four meals a day until he is about nine months old, then you can cut back to two daily meals for the rest of his life. Two daily meals are better for a dog's digestion than one large one, and if your dog loves his food, he probably would prefer to have a breakfast and a dinner anyway.

FEEDING THE ADULT DOG

For the adult (meaning physically mature) dog, feeding properly is about maintenance, not growth. Again, correct weight is a concern. Your dog should appear fit and should have an evident "waist." His ribs should not be protruding (a sign of being underweight), but they should be covered by only a

Young English Cockers require a diet different from that of adult dogs. A good puppy diet promotes healthy growth and development, while the adult diet's goal is maintaining overall good health and condition.

slight layer of fat. Under normal circumstances, an adult dog can be maintained fairly easily with a high-quality, nutritionally complete adult-formula food.

Whatever you are going to feed your dog, don't rely entirely on the quantities given in the manufacturer's instructions on the package. Every dog has different requirements and—as in humans—where one dog will grow fat on just a small portion, another will need double the quantity to stay in fit condition. So it is best to "feed with your eyes."

Factor treats into your dog's overall daily caloric intake, and avoid offering table scraps. Not only are certain "people foods," like chocolate, onions, grapes, raisins and nuts, toxic to dogs, but feeding from the table also encourages begging and overeating. Overweight dogs are more prone to health problems. Research has even shown that obesity takes years off a dog's life. With that in mind, resist the urge to overfeed and over-treat. Don't make unnecessary additions to your

DIET DON'TS

- Got milk? Don't give it to your dog! Dogs cannot tolerate large quantities of cows' milk, as they do not have the enzymes to digest lactose.
- You may have heard of dog owners who add raw eggs to their dogs' food for a shiny coat or to make the food more palatable, but consumption of raw eggs too often can cause a deficiency of the vitamin biotin.
- Avoid feeding table scraps, as they will upset the balance of the dog's complete food. Additionally, fatty or highly seasoned foods can cause upset canine stomachs.
- Do not offer raw meat to your dog. Raw meat can contain parasites; it also is high in fat.
- Vitamin A toxicity in dogs can be caused by too much raw liver, especially if the dog already gets enough vitamin A in his balanced diet, which should be the case.
- Bones like chicken, pork chop and other soft bones are not suitable, as they easily splinter.

dog's diet, whether with tidbits or with extra vitamins and minerals. A good dog food will have complete nutrition in proper proportions, and you don't want to upset the balance. It's not a case of "if a little is good, a lot is better."

The amount of food needed for proper maintenance will vary depending on the individual dog's activity level, but you will be able to tell whether the daily portions are keeping him in good shape. With the wide variety of good complete foods available, choosing what to feed is largely a matter of personal preference. Just as with the puppy, the adult dog should have consistency in his mealtimes and feeding place. In addition to a consistent routine, regular mealtimes also allow the owner to see how much his dog is eating. If the dog seems never to be satisfied or, likewise, becomes uninterested in his food, the owner will know right away that something is wrong and can consult the vet.

DIETS FOR THE AGING DOG

A good rule of thumb is that once a dog has reached around 75% of his expected lifespan, he has reached "senior citizen" or geriatric status. Your English Cocker Spaniel will be considered a senior at about 9 years of age; based on his size, he has a projected lifespan of about 12–14 years. (The smallest breeds generally enjoy the longest lives and the largest breeds the shortest.)

What does aging have to do with your dog's diet? No, he won't get a discount at the local diner's early-bird special. Yes, he will require some dietary changes to accommodate the changes that come along with increased age. One change is that the older dog's

SWITCHING FOODS

There are certain times in a dog's life when it becomes necessary to switch his food; for example, from puppy to adult food and then from adult to senior-dog food. Additionally, you may decide to feed your pup a different type of food from what he received from the breeder, and there may be "emergency" situations in which you can't find your dog's normal brand and have to offer something else temporarily. Anytime a change is made, for whatever reason, the switch must be done gradually. You don't want to upset the dog's stomach or end up with a picky eater who refuses to eat something new. A tried-and-true approach is, over the course of about a week, to mix a little of the new food in with the old, increasing the proportion of new to old as the days progress. At the end of the week, you'll be feeding his regular portions of the new food, and he will barely notice the change.

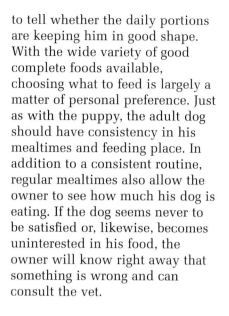

FEEDING IN HOT WEATHER

Even the most dedicated chow hound may have less of an appetite when the weather is hot or humid. If your dog leaves more of his food behind than usual, adjust his portions until the weather and his appetite return to normal. Never leave the uneaten portion in the bowl hoping he will return to finish it, because higher temperatures encourage food spoilage and bacterial growth.

WATER

Just as your dog needs proper nutrition from his food, water is an essential "nutrient" as well. Water keeps the dog's body properly hydrated and promotes normal function of the body's systems. During housebreaking it is necessary to keep an eye on how much water your English Cocker is drinking, but once he is reliably trained he should have access to clean fresh water at all times. Make sure that the dog's water bowl is clean, and change the water often.

You will find that your English Cocker Spaniel is a very sloppy drinker! He loves his water bowl and in his enthusiasm he will often put not only his mouth but also both front paws in the bowl, or he will take one last mouthful of water and, before swallowing it, come to you to tell you how much he loves you! A special spaniel bowl may help you keep the kitchen floor clean; this bowl is designed to keep long ears out of the food and water.

dietary needs become more similar to that of a puppy. Specifically, dogs can metabolize more protein as youngsters and seniors than in the adult-maintenance stage. Discuss with your vet whether you need to switch to a higher-protein or senior-formulated food or whether your current adult-dog food contains sufficient nutrition for the senior.

Watching the dog's weight remains essential, even more so in the senior stage. Older dogs are already more vulnerable to illness, and obesity only contributes to their susceptibility to problems. As the older dog becomes less active and thus exercises less, his regular portions may cause him to gain weight. At this point, you may consider decreasing his daily food intake or switching to a reduced-calorie food. As with other changes, you should consult your veterinarian for advice.

Spending a day in the field, hunting and retrieving, requires great stamina and strength. Although your English Cocker may not get the chance to hunt, he still needs adequate outlets for exercise and entertainment.

Retrieving from land and water is every English Cocker's favorite pastime. The breed's coat is designed to withstand the water and provide insulation.

EXERCISE

All dogs require some form of exercise, regardless of breed. A sedentary lifestyle is as harmful to a dog as it is to a person. The English Cocker Spaniel is a very lively and active breed that requires a lot of free exercise. He will enjoy on-lead walks and will like to accompany you to different places, but what he needs is free running, preferably in exciting surroundings like woods or fields, of course under your supervision and at a safe calling distance.

Owners often make mistakes in the exercise they give their dogs. Whereas the new puppy is an exciting thing, they tend to give him too much exercise. Of course you will be excited to bring your pup out and about, around the neighborhood, to meet new friends, but it means that the small puppy is taken on too many walks. For a puppy up to six months old, the yard is big enough. Take him to the dog park once a day to let him socialize and play with the other dogs for about 15 minutes. Once the puppy

WEIGHT AND SEE!

When you look at yourself in the mirror each day, you get very used to what you see! It's only when you pull out last year's holiday outfit and can't zip it up that you notice that you've put on some pounds. Dog owners are the same way with their dogs. Often a few pounds go unnoticed, and it's not until some time passes or the vet remarks that your dog looks more than pleasantly plump that you realize what's happened. To avoid your pet's becoming obese right under your very nose, make a habit of routinely evaluating his condition with a hands-on test.

Can you feel, but not see, your dog's rib cage? Does your dog have a waist? His waist should be evident by touch and also visible from above and from the side. In top view, the dog's body should have an hourglass shape. These are indicators of good condition.

While it's not hard to spot an extremely skinny or overly rotund dog, it's the subtle changes that lead up to under- or overweight condition of which we must be aware. If your dog's ribs are visible, he is too thin. Conversely, if you can't feel the ribs under too much fat, and if there's no indication of a waistline, your dog is overweight. Both of these conditions require changes to the diet. A trip or sometimes just a call to the vet will help you modify your dog's feeding.

is about nine months old, you can extend his daily walks to about an hour long, and once he is a year old his energy will be boundless.

We cannot stress the importance of proper exercise enough. It is essential to keep the dog's body fit, but it is also essential to his mental well-being. A bored dog will find something to do, which often manifests itself in some type of destructive behavior. In this sense, it is essential for *your* mental well-being!

GROOMING YOUR COCKER

BRUSHING
A natural bristle brush or a slicker brush can be used for regular routine brushing. Daily brushing is effective for removing

dead hair and stimulating the dog's natural oils to add shine and a healthy look to the coat. Also, the soft and silky spaniel coat can easily form tangles and mats, especially in places like the "armpits" and behind the ears, and it is important to prevent these from forming.

TRIMMING AND PRESENTATION
When you buy your puppy he will have a smooth, short coat without much feathering, but by the time your puppy is five or six months old you'll find that he starts looking more like an Afghan Hound than an English Cocker Spaniel! The coat grows fluffy, the feathering gets longer and he will

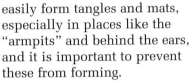

Introduce the English Cocker puppy to grooming at an early age. Make your daily brushing sessions fun for the puppy.

Much of the English Cocker is hand-stripped, but scissors are used sparingly in certain places.

Selecting the best grooming tools is essential with English Cockers. A slicker brush is ideal for removing dead hair and tangles from your dog's coat.

have a big topknot on his head and a long flag on his tail. With all of the hair on his feet, he will bring a lot of mud and dirt into the house.

You must always remember that the coat of an English Cocker Spaniel is to be hand-stripped only. Clipping and razoring is

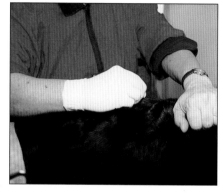

A thin rubber glove or rubber fingertips assist in stripping the dead hairs from the dog's coat. The gloves keep the hair from sliding through your fingers.

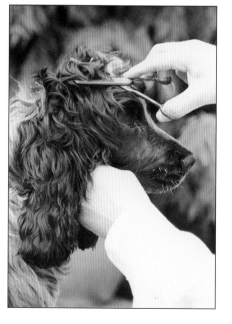

The ears require a combination of hand-plucking, trimming with thinning shears as well as attention to the hair inside the ears. Excess hair can cause ear problems and should be removed.

absolutely out of the question, since it destroys the density of color and you will never get that lovely silky sheen that you get when you hand-strip the coat.

If you think you are not up to this job, you'll have to seek help. Ask the breeder whether he can help you; sometimes breeders use their (little) spare time to groom. If not, you'll have to take your puppy to a professional groomer with experience in hand-stripping. Be very careful where you go, since grooming parlors often believe that their canine clients want nothing but to have all of their excess hair removed—and that means that the featherings on his legs go, his back is clippered and the beautiful feathering on the ears is cut off. You have to stress the fact that what you want is a show trim—your English Cocker must be shaped in the way in which he looks his best and this should be done by hand-plucking and not by scissoring or clippering.

The puppy's coat may take some time to get ready to come out; sometimes you have to wait until the puppy is eight or nine months old. This is annoying when you want to show the puppy, but be patient! Don't hurry the coat by using cutting instruments; you will regret that later.

What you should do in the meantime is groom your puppy

regularly so that he is quite used to being on a table and being handled. Also, the abundant hair around the feet and between the pads on the underside can be cut away.

When you find that your puppy's coat may be ready to come out, you may find it easier to remove the hair by using "thumblettes," which fit over your thumb and forefinger, or thin surgical gloves, which are quite tight-fitting.

Start with the head. Gently pull out the long hair, always pulling in the direction that the hair grows. This sounds painful, but it is not, since what you pull out is dead hair. Start with just a couple of hairs so that your puppy can get used to the feel and so that you will not run the risk of hurting him by pulling out too many hairs at the same time. If you have a really smooth finish on top of the head, go to the top of the ears and remove the long hairs there, shaping around the back of the ear and about one-third of the way down. With your thinning scissors, cut carefully under the corner of the ear next to the head, and then thin out all long and surplus hair from the breastbone up to and including the throat.

Vets will often tell you that English Cockers always have ear problems. This is not true. As long as you keep the inside of the ear clean and free of hair so that the ear can "breathe" and, if necessary, use ear cleaner, you will find that you will have no problems with your English Cocker's ears.

The coat on the neck must be stripped out as short as possible, also with your finger and thumb. If you use a fine-tooth comb regularly, you will find that it will remove nearly all of the puppy fluff. Try to use the comb as a stripping tool by gripping the hair between the comb and your thumb and pulling it toward you. It helps when you weave an elastic band between the teeth of the comb.

Continue down the shoulders until they are smooth and clear.

Serrated scissors or thinning shears, as they are often called, are used to thin out excess hair and create a pleasing outline on your English Cocker.

Trimming the feet is difficult and must be done with care. Always cut the hair in the direction of the toes and follow the outline of the foot closely.

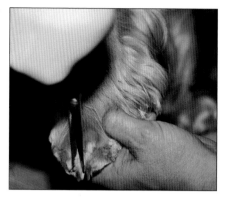

Start with lifting the foot and cutting out all the surplus hair from underneath. Cut closely around the outline of the foot. Then put the foot down and cut the surplus hair away that sticks up between the toes. Cut in the direction of the toes. Do not cut away the hair in between the toes, since that makes the foot look like a splayed foot. Finish off with a good brush and you will find that instead of a bundle of fluff, you now have an English Cocker with

The forelegs will have a lot of fluffy hair on the sides and the front. This must be removed. The feathering on the backsides of the front legs stays as it is. The feathering should not touch the ground; when it does, you can shape it with scissors. When viewed from the front, the feathering should lie backwards quite naturally from the elbow.

Work the comb with the elastic band through the body coat, the hair on the ribs and the outside of the hind legs. Pluck out the fluffy hair that will not come out with the comb. Leave the feathering around the stifles. Trim the tail and cut underneath it. Pluck the hair down to where the feathering falls downwards and trim the feathering into shape. Shape the hair on the hocks with the thinning scissors but do not take too much hair away; the hocks should look full.

Trimming the feet is not easy and you have to be very careful.

WATER SHORTAGE

No matter how well behaved your dog is, bathing is always a project! Nothing can substitute for a good warm bath, but owners do have the option of giving their dogs "dry" baths. Pet shops sell excellent products, in both powder and spray forms, designed for spot-cleaning your dog. These dry shampoos are convenient for touch-up jobs when you don't have the time to bathe your dog in the traditional way.

Muddy feet, messy behinds and smelly coats can be spot-cleaned and deodorized with a "wet-nap"-style cleaner. On those days when your dog insists on rolling in fresh goose droppings and there's no time for a bath, a spot bath can save the day. These pre-moistened wipes are also handy for other grooming needs like wiping faces, ears and eyes and freshening tails and behinds.

a beautiful smooth and shining coat, gleaming with health and good condition.

Bathing

Dogs do not need to be bathed as often as humans, but sometimes a bath will be necessary. It is therefore important that you accustom your pup to being bathed as a puppy so that he is used to it when he grows up. You will have to bathe your dog the day before a show, and most owners like to bathe their bitches after they have been in season.

Before you bathe your dog, make sure that the coat is absolutely tangle-free. Have the items you'll need close at hand. First, decide where you will bathe the dog. You should have a tub or basin with a non-slip surface. Puppies can even be bathed in a sink. In warm weather, some like to use a portable pool in the yard, although you'll want to make sure your dog doesn't head for the nearest dirt pile following his bath! You will also need a hose or shower spray to wet the coat thoroughly, a shampoo formulated for dogs, absorbent towels and perhaps a blow dryer. Human shampoos are too harsh for dogs' coats and will dry them out.

Before wetting the dog, give him a brush-through to remove any dead hair, dirt and mats. Make sure he is at ease in the tub and have the water at a comfortable

Pet shops sell special clippers for use on dogs' nails. These nail clippers assist you in not cutting into the "quick," the vein running through the nail.

temperature. Begin bathing by wetting the coat all the way down to the skin. Massage in the shampoo, keeping it away from his face and eyes. Rinse him thoroughly, again avoiding the eyes and ears, as you don't want to get water into the ear canals. A thorough rinsing is important, as shampoo residue is drying and itchy to the dog. After rinsing, wrap him in a towel to absorb the initial moisture. You can finish drying with either a towel or a blow dryer on low heat, held at a safe distance from the dog and brushing as you dry. You should keep the dog indoors and away from any drafts until he is completely dry.

Nail Clipping

Having their nails trimmed is not on many dogs' lists of favorite things to do. With this in mind, you will need to accustom your

Routine ear cleaning should be done gently with a soft cotton wipe or cotton ball. Should you find evidence of parasites, blood, or waxy discharge, contact your vet immediately.

light, and what better way to convince him than with food? You may want to enlist the help of an assistant to comfort the pup and offer treats as you concentrate on the clipping itself. The guillotine-type clipper is thought of by many as the easiest type to use; the nail tip is inserted into the opening, and blades on the top and bottom snip it off in one clip.

Start by grasping the pup's paw; a little pressure on the foot

puppy to the procedure at a young age so that he will sit still (well, as still as he can) for his pedicures. Long nails can cause the dog's feet to spread, which is not good for him; likewise, long nails can hurt if they unintentionally scratch, not good for you!

Some dogs' nails are worn down naturally by regular walking on hard surfaces, so the frequency with which you clip depends on your individual dog. Look at his nails from time to time and clip as needed; a good way to know when it's time for a trim is if you hear your dog clicking as he walks across the floor.

There are several types of nail clippers and even electric nail-grinding tools made for dogs. First we'll discuss using the clipper. To start, have your clipper ready and some doggie treats on hand. You want your pup to view his nail-clipping sessions in a positive

SCOOTING HIS BOTTOM

Here's a doggy problem that many owners tend to neglect. If your dog is scooting his rear end around the carpet, he probably is experiencing anal-sac impaction or blockage. The anal sacs are the two grape-sized glands on either side of the dog's vent. The dog cannot empty these glands, which become filled with a foul-smelling material. The dog may attempt to lick the area to relieve the pressure. He may also rub his anus on your walls, furniture or floors.

Don't neglect your dog's rear end during grooming sessions. By squeezing both sides of the anus with a soft cloth, you can express some of the material in the sacs. If the material is pasty and thick, you likely will need the assistance of a veterinarian. Vets know how to express the glands and can show you how to do it correctly without hurting the dog or spraying yourself with the unpleasant liquid.

pad causes the nail to extend, making it easier to clip. Clip off a little at a time. If you can see the "quick," which is a blood vessel that runs through each nail, you will know how much to trim, as you do not want to cut into the quick. On that note, if you do cut the quick, which will cause bleeding, you can stem the flow of blood with a styptic pencil or other clotting agent. If you mistakenly nip the quick, do not panic or fuss, as this will cause the pup to be afraid. Simply reassure the pup, stop the bleeding and move on to the next nail. Don't be discouraged; you will become a professional canine pedicurist with practice.

You may or may not be able to see the quick, so it's best to just clip off a small bit at a time. If you see a dark dot in the center of the nail, this is the quick and your cue to stop clipping. Tell the puppy he's a "good boy" and offer a piece of treat with each nail. You can also use nail-clipping time to examine the footpads, making sure that they are not dry and cracked and that nothing has become embedded in them.

If you are wary of using nail clippers, you might prefer the use of a nail grinder. This is a small battery-operated contraption that slowly grinds the nails. There is no fear of cutting into the quick and the dogs don't usually mind the slight buzzing sound of the grinder

Ears can be cleaned with an ear cleaner made specifically for dogs. If you are attentive to your English Cocker's ears, he should not be plagued by ear problems.

at all, although you must be careful not to catch any of the coat in the grinder.

EAR CLEANING

While keeping your dog's ears clean unfortunately will not cause him to "hear" your commands any better, it will protect him from ear infection and ear-mite infestation. In addition, a dog's ears are vulnerable to waxy build-up and to collecting foreign matter from the outdoors. Look in your dog's ears regularly to ensure that they look pink, clean and otherwise healthy. Even if they look fine, an odor in the ears signals a problem and means it's time to call the vet.

A dog's ears should be cleaned regularly; once a week is suggested, and you can do this along with your regular brushing. Using a cotton ball or pad, and never probing into the ear canal, wipe the ear gently. You can use an ear-cleansing liquid or powder available from your vet or pet-supply store; alternatively, you might prefer to use home-made solutions with ingredients like one part white vinegar and one part hydrogen peroxide. Ask your vet about home remedies before you attempt to concoct something on your own!

Keep your dog's ears free of excess hair by plucking the hair as needed. If done gently, this will be painless for the dog. Look for wax, brown droppings (a sign of ear mites), redness or any other abnormalities. If your English Cocker Spaniel has been shaking his head or scratching at his ears frequently, this usually indicates a problem. In this case, don't clean the ear canal yourself. If you poke into the ear canal with tweezers or cotton swab, you'll only succeed in aggravating things and could injure your dog in the process. Contact your vet before the condition gets serious.

If you check your spaniel's ears regularly and use ear cleaner to keep his ears clean, you will find that the English Cocker's reputation for ear trouble is totally unfounded.

EYE CARE

During grooming sessions, pay extra attention to the condition of your dog's eyes. If the area around the eyes is soiled or if tear staining has occurred, there are various cleaning agents made especially for this purpose. Look at the dog's eyes to make sure no debris has

entered; dogs who spend lots of time outdoors are especially prone to this.

The signs of an eye infection are obvious: mucus, redness, puffiness, scabs or other signs of irritation. If your dog's eyes become infected, the vet will likely prescribe an antibiotic ointment for treatment. If you notice signs of more serious problems, such as opacities in the eye, which usually indicate cataracts, consult the vet at once. Taking time to pay attention to your dog's eyes will alert you in the early stages of any problem so that you can get your dog treatment as soon as possible. You could save your dog's sight!

ID FOR YOUR COCKER

You love your English Cocker Spaniel and want to keep him safe. Of course you take every precaution to prevent his escaping from

---

PET OR STRAY?

Besides the obvious benefit of providing your contact information to whoever finds your lost dog, an ID tag makes your dog more approachable and more likely to be recovered. A strange dog wandering the neighborhood without a collar and tags will look like a stray, while the collar and tags indicate that the dog is someone's pet. Even if the ID tags become detached from the collar, the collar alone will make a person more likely to pick up the dog.

the yard or becoming lost or stolen. You have a sturdy high fence and you always keep your dog on lead when out and about in public places. If your dog is not properly identified, however, you are overlooking a major aspect of his safety. We hope to never be in a situation where our dog is missing, but we should practice prevention in the unfortunate case that this happens; identification greatly increases the chances of your dog's being returned to you.

Show your English Cocker how much you love him by making sure he is properly identified and always providing for his safety.

There are several ways to identify your dog. First, the traditional dog tag should be a staple in your dog's wardrobe, attached to his everyday collar. Tags can be made of sturdy plastic and various metals and should include your contact information so that a person who finds the dog can get in touch with you right away to arrange his return. Many people today enjoy the wide range of decorative tags available, so have fun and create a tag to match your dog's personality. Of course, it is important that the tag stays on the collar, so have a secure "O" ring attachment; you also can explore the type of tag that slides right onto the collar.

In addition to the ID tag, which every dog should wear even if identified by another method, two other forms of identification have become popular: microchipping and tattooing. In microchipping, a tiny scannable chip is painlessly inserted under the dog's skin. The number is registered to you so that if your lost dog turns up at a clinic or shelter, the chip can be scanned to retrieve your contact information.

The advantage of the microchip is that it is a permanent form of ID, but there are some factors to consider. Several different companies make microchips, and not all are compatible with the others' scanning devices. It's best to find a company with a universal microchip that can be read by scanners made by other companies as well. It won't do any good to have the dog chipped if the information cannot be retrieved. Also, not every humane society, shelter and clinic is equipped with a scanner, although more and more facilities are equipping themselves. In fact,

CAR CAUTION

You may like to bring your canine companion along on the daily errands, but if you will be running in and out from place to place and can't bring him indoors with you, leave him at home. Your dog should never be left alone in the car, not even for a minute—never! A car heats up very quickly, and even a cracked-open window will not help. In fact, leaving the window cracked will be dangerous if the dog becomes uncomfortable and tries to escape. When in doubt, leave your dog home, where you know he will be safe.

many shelters microchip dogs that they adopt out to new homes.

Because the microchip is not visible to the eye, the dog must wear a tag that states that he is microchipped so that whoever picks him up will know to have him scanned. He of course also should have a tag with contact information in case his chip cannot be read. Humane societies and veterinary clinics offer this service, which is usually very affordable.

Though less popular than microchipping, tattooing is another permanent method of ID for dogs. Most vets perform this service, and there are also clinics that perform dog tattooing. This is also an affordable procedure and one that will not cause much discomfort for the dog. It is best to put the tattoo in a visible area, such as the ear, to deter theft. It is sad to say that there are cases of dogs' being stolen and sold to research laboratories, but such laboratories will not accept tattooed dogs.

To ensure that the tattoo is effective in aiding your dog's return to you, the tattoo number must be registered with a national organization. That way, when someone finds a tattooed dog a phone call to the registry will match the dog with his owner.

Your English Cocker should have a permanent form of ID like a microchip or tattoo for safety's sake. This is an example of a tattoo on the inside of the thigh.

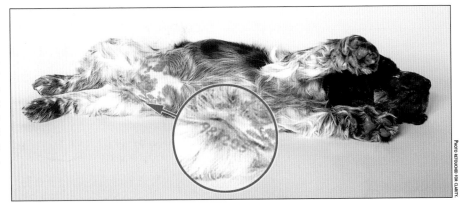

ENGLISH COCKER SPANIEL

BASIC TRAINING PRINCIPLES: PUPPY VS. ADULT

There's a big difference between training an adult dog and training a young puppy. With a young puppy, everything is new. At eight to ten weeks of age, he will be experiencing many things, and he has nothing with which to compare these experiences. Up to this point, he has been with his dam and littermates, not one-on-one with people except in his interactions with his breeder and visitors to the litter.

When you first bring the puppy home, he is eager to please you. This means that he accepts doing things your way. During the next couple of months, he will absorb the basis of everything he needs to know for the rest of his life. This early age is even referred to as the "sponge" stage. After that, for the next 18 months, it's up to you to reinforce good manners by building on the foundation that you've established. Once your puppy is reliable in basic commands and behavior and has reached the

appropriate age, you may gradually introduce him to some of the interesting sports, games and activities available to pet owners and their dogs.

Raising your puppy is a family affair. Each member of the family must know what rules to set forth for the puppy and how to use the same one-word commands to

With a future show dog, training for the ring starts early. In addition to the basics, the pup should learn to stand/stay and also stand on a table for examination.

mean exactly the same thing every time. Even if yours is a large family, one person will soon be considered by the pup to be the leader, the Alpha person in his pack, the "boss" who must be obeyed. Often that highly regarded person turns out to be the one who feeds the puppy. Food ranks very

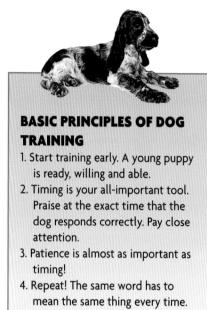

BASIC PRINCIPLES OF DOG TRAINING

1. Start training early. A young puppy is ready, willing and able.
2. Timing is your all-important tool. Praise at the exact time that the dog responds correctly. Pay close attention.
3. Patience is almost as important as timing!
4. Repeat! The same word has to mean the same thing every time.
5. In the beginning, praise all correct behavior verbally, along with treats and petting.

high on the puppy's list of important things! That's why your puppy is rewarded with small treats along with verbal praise when he responds to you correctly. As the puppy learns to do what you want him to do, the food rewards are gradually eliminated and only the praise remains. If you were to keep up with the food treats, you could have two problems on your hands—an obese dog and a beggar.

Training begins the minute your English Cocker Spaniel puppy steps through the doorway of your home, so don't make the

You cannot stop a Cocker Spaniel from having fun and following his inborn retrieving instinct. His abilities might just surprise you!

mistake of putting the puppy on the floor and telling him by your actions to "Go for it! Run wild!" Even if this is your first puppy, you must act as if you know what you're doing: be the boss. An uncertain pup may be terrified to move, while a bold one will be ready to take you at your word and start plotting to destroy the house! Before you collected your puppy, you decided where his own special place would be, and that's where to put him when you first arrive home. Give him a house tour after he has investigated his area and had a nap and a bathroom "pit stop."

It's worth mentioning here that if you've adopted an adult dog that is completely trained to your liking, lucky you! You're off the hook! However, if that dog spent his life up to this point in a kennel, or even in a good home but without any real training, be prepared to tackle the job ahead. A

CREATURES OF HABIT

Canine behaviorists and trainers aptly describe dogs as "creatures of habit," meaning that dogs respond to structure in their daily lives and welcome a routine. Do not interpret this to mean that dogs enjoy endless repetition in their training sessions. Dogs get bored just as humans do. Keep training sessions interesting and exciting. Vary the commands and the locations in which you practice. Give short breaks for play in between lessons. A bored student will never be the best performer in the class.

dog three years of age or older with no previous training cannot be blamed for not knowing what he was never taught. While the dog is trying to understand and learn your rules, at the same time he has to unlearn many of his previously self-taught habits and general view of the world.

Working with a professional trainer will speed up your progress with an adopted adult dog. You'll need patience, too. Some new rules may be close to impossible for the dog to accept. After all, he's been successful so far by doing everything his way! (Patience again.) He may agree with your instruction for a few days and then slip back into his old ways, so you must be just as consistent and understanding in your teaching as you would be

with a puppy. (More patience needed yet again!) Your dog has to learn to pay attention to your voice, your family, the daily routine, new smells, new sounds and, in some cases, even a new climate.

One of the most important things to find out about a newly adopted adult dog is his reaction to children (yours and others), strangers and your friends, and how he acts upon meeting other dogs. If he was not socialized with dogs as a puppy, this could be a major problem. This does not mean that he's a "bad" dog, a vicious dog or an aggressive dog; rather, it means that he has no idea how to read another dog's body language. There's no way for him to tell whether the other dog is a friend or foe. Survival instinct takes over, telling him to attack first and ask questions later. This definitely calls for professional help and, even then, may not be a behavior that can be corrected 100% reliably (or even at all). If you have a puppy, this is why it is so very important to introduce your young puppy properly to other puppies and "dog-friendly" adult dogs.

HOUSE-TRAINING YOUR ENGLISH COCKER SPANIEL

Dogs are tactility-oriented when it comes to house-training. In other words, they respond to the surface on which they are given approval

SOMEBODY TO BLAME

House-training a puppy can be frustrating for the puppy and the owner alike. The puppy does not instinctively understand the difference between defecating on the pavement outside and on the ceramic tile in the kitchen. He is confused and frightened by his human's exuberant reactions to his natural urges. The owner, arguably the more intelligent of the duo, is also frustrated that he cannot convince his puppy to obey his commands and instructions.

In frustration, the owner may struggle with the temptation to discipline the puppy, scold him or even strike him on the rear end. Harsh corrections are unnecessary and inappropriate, serving to defeat your purpose in gaining your puppy's trust and respect. Don't blame your nine-week-old puppy. Blame yourself for not being 100% consistent in the puppy's lessons and routine. The lesson here is simple: try harder and your puppy will succeed.

to eliminate. The choice is yours (the dog's version is in parentheses): The lawn (including the neighbors' lawns)? A bare patch of earth under a tree (where people like to sit and relax in the summertime)? Concrete steps or patio (all sidewalks, garages and basement floors)? The curbside (watch out for cars)? A small area of crushed stone in a corner of the yard (mine!)? The latter is the best choice if you can manage it, because it will remain strictly for the dog's use and is very easy to keep clean.

You can start out with paper-training indoors and switch over to an outdoor surface as the puppy matures and gains control over his need to eliminate. For the nay-sayers, don't worry—this won't mean that the dog will soil on every piece of newspaper lying around the house. You are training him to go outside, remember? Starting out by paper-training is sometimes the only choice for a city dog.

WHEN YOUR PUPPY'S "GOT TO GO"
Your puppy's need to relieve himself is seemingly non-stop, but signs of improvement will be seen each week. From 8 to 10 weeks old, the puppy will have to be taken outside every time he wakes up, about 10–15 minutes after every meal and after every period of play—all day long, from first thing in the morning until his bedtime! That's a total of ten or more trips per day to teach the puppy where it's okay to relieve himself. With that schedule in mind, you can see that house-training a young puppy is not a part-time job. It requires someone to be home all day.

If that seems overwhelming or impossible, do a little planning. For example, plan to pick up your puppy at the start of a vacation

CANINE DEVELOPMENT SCHEDULE

It is important to understand how and at what age a puppy develops into adulthood.
If you are a puppy owner, consult the following Canine Development Schedule to
determine the stage of development your puppy is currently experiencing.
This knowledge will help you as you work with the puppy in the weeks and months ahead.

PERIOD	AGE	CHARACTERISTICS
FIRST TO THIRD	BIRTH TO SEVEN WEEKS	Puppy needs food, sleep and warmth and responds to simple and gentle touching. Needs mother for security and disciplining. Needs littermates for learning and interacting with other dogs. Pup learns to function within a pack and learns pack order of dominance. Begin socializing pup with adults and children for short periods. Pup begins to become aware of his environment.
FOURTH	EIGHT TO TWELVE WEEKS	Brain is fully developed. Pup needs socializing with outside world. Remove from mother and littermates. Needs to change from canine pack to human pack. Human dominance necessary. Fear period occurs between 8 and 12 weeks. Avoid fright and pain.
FIFTH	THIRTEEN TO SIXTEEN WEEKS	Training and formal obedience should begin. Less association with other dogs, more with people, places, situations. Period will pass easily if you remember this is pup's change-to-adolescence time. Be firm and fair. Flight instinct prominent. Permissiveness and over-disciplining can do permanent damage. Praise for good behavior.
JUVENILE	FOUR TO EIGHT MONTHS	Another fear period about 7 to 8 months of age. It passes quickly, but be cautious of fright and pain. Sexual maturity reached. Dominant traits established. Dog should understand sit, down, come and stay by now.

NOTE: THESE ARE APPROXIMATE TIME FRAMES. ALLOW FOR INDIVIDUAL DIFFERENCES IN PUPPIES.

period. If you can't get home in the middle of the day, plan to hire a dog-sitter or ask a neighbor to come over to take the pup outside, feed him his lunch and then take him out again about ten or so minutes after he's eaten. Also make arrangements with that or another person to be your "emergency" contact if you have to stay late on the job. Remind yourself—repeatedly—that this hectic schedule improves as the puppy gets older.

HOME WITHIN A HOME

Your English Cocker Spaniel puppy needs to be confined to one secure, puppy-proof area when no one is able to watch his every move. Generally the kitchen is the place of choice because the floor is washable. Likewise, it's a busy family area that will accustom the pup to a variety of noises, everything from pots and pans to the telephone, blender and dishwasher. He will also be enchanted by the smell of your cooking (and will never be critical when you burn something). An exercise pen (also called an "ex-pen," a puppy version of a playpen) within the room of choice is an excellent means of confinement for a young pup. He can see out and has a certain amount of space in which to run about, but he is safe from dangerous things like electrical cords, heating units, trash baskets or open kitchen-supply cabinets. Place the pen where the puppy will not get a blast of heat or air conditioning.

In the pen, you can put a few toys, his bed (which can be his crate if the dimensions of pen and crate are compatible) and a few layers of newspaper in one small corner, just in case. A water bowl can be hung at a convenient height on the side of the ex-pen so it won't become a splashing pool for an innovative puppy. His food dish can go on the floor, near but not under the water bowl.

Crates are something that pet owners are at last getting used to for their dogs. Wild or domestic canines have always preferred to sleep in den-like safe spots, and

DAILY SCHEDULE

How many relief trips does your puppy need per day? A puppy up to the age of 14 weeks will need to go outside about 8 to 12 times per day! You will have to take the pup out any time he starts sniffing around the floor or turning in small circles, as well as after naps, meals, games and lessons or whenever he's released from his crate. Once the puppy is 14 to 22 weeks of age, he will require only 6 to 8 relief trips. At the ages of 22 to 32 weeks, the puppy will require about 5 to 7 trips. Adult dogs typically require 4 relief trips per day, in the morning, afternoon, evening and late at night.

that is exactly what the crate provides. How often have you seen adult dogs that choose to sleep under a table or chair even though they have full run of the house? It's the den connection.

In your "happy" voice, use the word "Crate" every time you put the pup into his den. If he's new to a crate, toss in a small biscuit for him to chase the first few times. At night, after he's been outside, he should sleep in his crate. The crate may be kept in his designated area at night or, if you want to be sure to hear those wake-up yips in the morning, put the crate in a corner of your bedroom. However, don't make any response whatsoever to whining or crying. If he's completely ignored, he'll settle down and get to sleep.

Good bedding for a young puppy is an old folded bath towel or an old blanket, something that is easily washable and disposable if necessary ("accidents" will

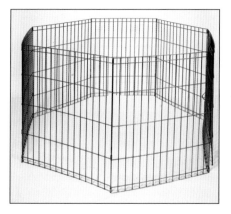

> ### EXTRA! EXTRA!
> The headlines read: "Puppy Piddles Here!" Breeders commonly use newspapers to line their whelping pens, so puppies learn to associate newspapers with relieving themselves. Do not use newspapers to line your pup's crate, as this will signal to your puppy that it is OK to urinate in his crate. If you choose to paper-train your puppy, you will layer newspapers on a section of the floor near the door he uses to go outside. You should encourage the puppy to use the papers to relieve himself, and bring him there whenever you see him getting ready to go. Little by little, you will reduce the size of the newspaper-covered area so that the puppy will learn to relieve himself "on the other side of the door."

happen!). Never put newspaper in the puppy's crate. Also those old ideas about adding a clock to replace his mother's heartbeat, or a hot-water bottle to replace her warmth, are just that—old ideas. The clock could drive the puppy nuts, and the hot-water bottle could end up as a very soggy waterbed! An extremely good breeder would have introduced your puppy to the crate by letting two pups sleep together for a couple of nights, followed by several nights alone. How thankful you will be if you found that breeder!

A wire "ex-pen," sturdy enough that a pup can't knock it down and high enough that a pup can't climb out, is useful for safely confining your puppy.

LEASH TRAINING

House-training and leash training go hand in hand, literally. When taking your puppy outside to do his business, lead him there on his leash. Unless an emergency potty run is called for, do not whisk the puppy up into your arms and take him outside. If you have a fenced yard, you have the advantage of letting the puppy loose to go out, but it's better to put the dog on the leash and take him to his designated place in the yard until he is reliably house-trained. Taking the puppy for a walk is the best way to house-train a dog. The dog will associate the walk with his time to relieve himself, and the exercise of walking stimulates the dog's bowels and bladder. Dogs that are not trained to relieve themselves on a walk may hold it until they get back home, which of course defeats half the purpose of the walk.

Safe toys in the pup's crate or area will keep him occupied, but monitor their condition closely. Discard any toys that show signs of being chewed to bits. Squeaky parts, bits of stuffing or plastic or any other small pieces can cause intestinal blockage or possibly choking if swallowed.

PROGRESSING WITH POTTY-TRAINING

After you've taken your puppy out and he has relieved himself in the area you've selected, he can have some free time with the family as long as there is someone responsible for watching him. That doesn't mean just someone in the same room who is watching TV or busy on the computer, but one person who is doing nothing other than keeping an eye on the pup, playing with him on the floor and helping him understand his position in the pack.

This first taste of freedom will let you begin to set the house rules. If you don't want the dog on the furniture, now is the time to prevent his first attempts to jump up onto the couch. The word to use in this case is "Off," not "Down." "Down" is the word you will use to teach the down position, which is something entirely different.

Most corrections at this stage come in the form of simply distracting the puppy. Instead of telling him "No" for "Don't chew the carpet," distract the chomping puppy with a toy and he'll forget about the carpet.

As you are playing with the pup, do not forget to watch him closely and pay attention to his body language. Whenever you see him begin to circle or sniff, take the puppy outside to relieve himself. If you are paper-training, put him back into his confined area on the newspapers. In either case, praise him as he eliminates while he actually is *in the act* of relieving himself. Three seconds after he has finished is too late!

You'll be praising him for running toward you, picking up a toy or whatever he may be doing at that moment, and that's not what you want to be praising him for. Timing is a vital tool in all dog training. Use it.

Remove soiled newspapers immediately and replace them with clean ones. You may want to take a small piece of soiled paper and place it in the middle of the new clean papers, as the scent will attract him to that spot when it's time to go again. That scent attraction is why it's so important to clean up any messes made in the house by using a product specially made to eliminate the odor of dog urine and droppings. Regular household cleansers won't do the trick. Pet shops sell the best pet deodorizers. Invest in the largest container you can find.

Scent attraction eventually will lead your pup to his chosen spot outdoors; this is the basis of outdoor training. When you take your puppy outside to relieve himself, use a one-word command such as "Outside" or "Go-potty" (that's one word to the puppy!) as you pick him up and attach his leash. Then put him down in his area. If he is too big for you to carry, snap the leash on quickly and lead him to his spot. Now comes the hard part—hard for you, that is. Just stand there until he urinates and defecates. Move him a few feet in one direction or

another if he's just sitting there looking at you, but remember that this is neither playtime nor time for a walk. This is strictly a business trip! Then, as he circles and squats (remember your timing!), give him a quiet "Good dog" as praise. If you start to jump for joy, ecstatic over his performance, he'll do one of two things: either he will stop mid-stream, as it were, or he'll do it again for you—in the house—and expect you to be just as delighted!

Give him five minutes or so and, if he doesn't go in that time,

Diligence in house-training your puppy results in a clean adult dog with whom it's a joy to share your home.

take him back indoors to his confined area and try again in another ten minutes, or immediately if you see him sniffing and circling. By careful observation, you'll soon work out a successful schedule.

Accidents, by the way, are just that—accidents. Clean them up quickly and thoroughly, without comment, after the puppy has been taken outside to finish his business and then put back into his area or crate. If you witness an accident in progress, say "No!" in a stern voice and get the pup outdoors immediately. No punishment is needed. You and your puppy are just learning each other's language, and sometimes it's easy to miss a puppy's message. Chalk it up to experience and watch more closely from now on.

KEEPING THE PACK ORDERLY

Discipline is a form of training that brings order to life. For example, military discipline is what allows the soldiers in an army to work as one. Discipline is a form of teaching and, in dogs, is the basis of how the successful pack operates. Each member knows his place in the pack and all respect the leader, or Alpha dog. It is essential for your puppy that you establish this type of relationship, with you as the Alpha, or leader. It is a form of social coexistence that all canines recognize and accept. Discipline, therefore, is never to be

---

POTTY COMMAND

Most dogs love to please their masters; there are no bounds to what dogs will do to make their owners happy. The potty command is a good example of this theory. If toileting on command makes the master happy, then more power to him. Puppies will obligingly piddle if it really makes their keepers smile. Some owners can be creative about which word they will use to command their dogs to relieve themselves. Some popular choices are "Potty," "Tinkle," "Piddle," "Let's go," "Hurry up" and "Toilet." Give the command every time your puppy goes into position and the puppy will begin to associate his business with the command.

---

confused with punishment. When you teach your puppy how you want him to behave, and he behaves properly and you praise him for it, you are disciplining him with a form of positive reinforcement.

For a dog, rewards come in the form of praise, a smile, a cheerful tone of voice, a few friendly pats or a rub of the ears. Rewards are also small food treats. Obviously, that does not mean bits of regular dog food. Instead, treats are very small bits of special things like cheese or pieces of soft dog treats. The idea is to reward the dog with something very small that he can taste and swallow, providing instant positive reinforcement. If he has to take time to chew the treat, he will have forgotten what he did to earn it by the time he is finished!

Your puppy should never be physically punished. The displeasure shown on your face and in your voice is sufficient to signal to the pup that he has done something wrong. He wants to please everyone higher up on the social ladder, especially his leader, so a scowl and harsh voice will take care of the error. Growling out the word "Shame!" when the pup is caught in the act of doing something wrong is better than the repetitive "No." Some dogs hear "No" so often that they begin to think it's their name! By the way, do not use the dog's name when you're correcting him. His name is reserved to get his attention for something pleasant about to take place.

There are punishments that have nothing to do with you. For example, your dog may think that chasing cats is one reason for his existence. You can try to stop it as much as you like but without success, because it's such fun for the dog. But one good hissing, spitting swipe of a cat's claws across the dog's nose will put an end to the game forever. Intervene only when your dog's eyeball is seriously at risk. Cat scratches can cause permanent damage to an innocent but annoying puppy.

PUPPY KINDERGARTEN

COLLAR AND LEASH
Before you begin your English Cocker Spaniel puppy's education, he must be used to his collar and leash. Choose a collar for your puppy that is secure, but not heavy or bulky. He won't enjoy training if he's uncomfortable. A flat buckle collar is fine for everyday wear and for initial puppy training. For older dogs, there are several types of training collars such as the martingale, which is a double loop that tightens slightly around the neck, or the head collar, which is similar to a horse's halter. A chain choke collar is not necessary for an English Cocker Spaniel. The breed needs to be trained consistently

---

WHO'S TRAINING WHOM?
Dog training is a black-and-white exercise. The correct response to a command must be absolute, and the trainer must insist on completely accurate responses from the dog. A trainer cannot command his dog to sit and then settle for the dog's melting into the down position. Often owners are so pleased that their dogs "did something" in response to a command that they just shrug and say, "OK, down" even though they wanted the dog to sit. You want your dog to respond to the command without hesitation; he must respond at that moment and correctly every time.

You must have your dog's attention before attempting to teach him anything. You won't accomplish anything if he is looking away from you, checking out the distractions around him.

but gently, and generally learns quickly and fares best with positive approaches.

A lightweight 6-foot woven cotton or nylon training leash is preferred by most trainers because it is easy to fold up in your hand and comfortable to hold because there is a certain amount of give to it. There are lessons where the dog will start off 6 feet away from you at the end of the leash. The leash used to take the puppy outside to relieve himself is shorter because you don't want him to roam away from his area. The shorter leash will also be the one to use initially when you walk the puppy.

If you've been wise enough to enroll in a puppy kindergarten training class, suggestions will be made as to the best collar and leash for your young puppy. I say "wise" because your puppy will be in a class with puppies in his

age range (up to five months old) of all breeds and sizes. It's the perfect way for him to learn the right way (and the wrong way) to interact with other dogs as well as their people. You cannot teach your puppy how to interpret another dog's sign language. For a first-time puppy owner, these socialization classes are extremely invaluable. For experienced dog owners, they are a real boon to further training.

ATTENTION

You've been using the dog's name since the minute you collected him from the breeder, so you should be able to get his attention by saying his name—with a big smile and in an excited tone of

SMILE WHEN YOU ORDER ME AROUND!

While trainers recommend practicing with your dog every day, it's perfectly acceptable to take a "mental health day" off. It's better not to train the dog on days when you're in a sour mood. Your bad attitude or lack of interest will be sensed by your dog, and he will respond accordingly. Studies show that dogs are well tuned in to their humans' emotions. Be conscious of how you use your voice when talking to your dog. Raising your voice or shouting will only erode your dog's trust in you as his trainer and master.

voice. His response will be the puppy equivalent of "Here I am! What are we going to do?" Your immediate response (if you haven't guessed by now) is "Good dog." Rewarding him at the moment he pays attention to you teaches him the proper way to respond when he hears his name.

For pup's safety, begin all lessons with the dog on-leash and only progress to off-leash training in enclosed areas. Start with no distractions to help keep his attention as he is learning.

EXERCISES FOR A BASIC CANINE EDUCATION

THE SIT EXERCISE

There are several ways to teach the Cocker puppy to sit. The first one is to catch him whenever he is about to sit and, as his backside nears the floor, say "Sit, good dog!" That's positive reinforcement and, if your timing is sharp, he will learn that what he's doing at that second is connected to your saying "Sit" and that you think he's clever for doing it!

Another method is to start with the puppy on his leash in front of you. Show him a treat in the palm of your right hand. Bring your hand up under his nose and, almost in slow motion, move your hand up and back so his nose goes up in the air and his head tilts back as he follows the treat in your hand. At that point, he will

have to either sit or fall over, so as his back legs buckle under, say "Sit, good dog," and then give him the treat and lots of praise. You may have to begin with your hand

Head up and bottom down is the basic principle of the sit position. Your dog may need to be guided into the correct position a few times but should get the idea quickly.

The English Cocker
demonstrates his
mastery of the
sit/stay by striking
a charming pose.

The English Cocker demonstrates his mastery of the sit/stay by striking a charming pose.

lightly running up his chest, actually lifting his chin up until he sits. Some (usually older) dogs require gentle pressure on their hindquarters with the left hand, in which case the dog should be on your left side. Puppies generally do not appreciate this physical dominance.

After a few times, you should be able to show the dog a treat in the open palm of your hand, raise your hand waist-high as you say "Sit" and have him sit. You thereby will have taught him two things at the same time. Both the verbal command and the motion of the hand are signals for the sit. Your puppy is watching you almost more than he is listening to you, so what you do is just as

important as what you say.

Don't save any of these drills only for training sessions. Use them as much as possible at odd times during a normal day. The dog should always sit before being given his food dish. He should sit to let you go through a doorway first, when the doorbell rings or when you stop to speak to someone on the street.

THE DOWN EXERCISE

Before beginning to teach the down command, you must consider how the dog feels about this exercise. To him, "down" is a submissive position. Being flat on the floor with you standing over him is not his idea of fun. It's up to you to let him know

READY, SIT, GO!

On your marks, get set: train! Most professional trainers agree that the sit command is the place to start your dog's formal education. Sitting is a natural posture for most dogs, and they respond to the sit exercise willingly and readily. For every lesson, begin with the sit command so that you start out with a successful exercise; likewise, you should practice the sit command at the end of every lesson as well because you always want to end on a high note.

SAY IT SIMPLY

When you command your dog to sit, use the word "Sit." Do not say "Sit down," as your dog will not know whether you mean "Sit" or "Down," or maybe you mean both. Be clear in your instructions to your dog; use one-word commands and always be consistent.

that, while it may not be fun, the reward of your approval is worth his effort.

Start with the puppy on your left side in a sit position. Hold the leash right above his collar in your left hand. Have an extra-special treat, such as a small piece of cooked chicken or hot dog, in your right hand. Place it at the end of the pup's nose and steadily move your hand down and forward along the ground. Hold the leash to prevent a sudden lunge for the food. As the puppy goes into the down position, say "Down" very gently.

The difficulty with this exercise is twofold: it's both the submissive aspect and the fact that most people say the word "Down" as if they were drill sergeants in charge of recruits! So issue the command sweetly, give him the treat and have the pup maintain the down position for several seconds. If he tries to get up immediately, place your hands on his shoulders and press down gently, giving him a very quiet

"Good dog." As you progress with this lesson, increase the "down time" until he will hold it until you say "Okay" (his cue for release). Practice this one in the house at various times throughout the day.

By increasing the length of time during which the dog must maintain the down position, you'll find many uses for it. For example, he can lie at your feet in the vet's office or anywhere that both of you have to wait, when you are on the phone, while the family is eating and so forth. If you progress to training for competitive obedience, he'll already be all set for the exercise called the "long down."

THE STAY EXERCISE

You can teach your English Cocker Spaniel to stay in the sit, down and stand positions. To teach the sit/stay, have the dog sit on your left side. Hold the leash at waist level in your left hand and let the dog know that you have a treat in your closed right hand. Step forward on your right foot as you say "Stay." Immediately turn and

As you teach the down command and gently guide your pup into position, make him feel comfortable and rewarded.

stand directly in front of the dog, keeping your right hand up high so he'll keep his eye on the treat hand and maintain the sit position for a count of five. Return to your original position and offer the reward.

Increase the length of the sit/stay each time until the dog can hold it for at least 30 seconds without moving. After about a week of success, move out on your right foot and take two steps before turning to face the dog. Give the "Stay" hand signal (left palm held up and facing the dog) as you leave. He gets the treat when you return and he holds the sit/stay. Increase the distance that you walk away from him before turning until you reach the length of your training leash. But don't rush it! Go back to the beginning if he moves before he should. No matter what the lesson, never be upset by having to go back to an easier lesson for a few days. The repetition and practice are what will make your dog reliable in these commands. It won't do any good to move on to something more difficult if the command is not mastered at the easier levels. Above all, even if you do get frustrated, never let your puppy know! Always keep a positive, upbeat attitude during training, which will transmit to your dog for positive results.

The down/stay is taught in the same way once the dog is

TIME TO PLAY!

Playtime can happen both indoors and out. A young puppy is growing so rapidly that he needs sleep more than he needs a lot of physical exercise. Puppies get sufficient exercise on their own just through normal puppy activity. Monitor play with young children so you can remove the puppy when he's had enough, or calm the kids if they get too rowdy. Almost all puppies love to chase after a toy you've thrown, and you can turn your games into educational activities. Every time your puppy brings the toy back to you, say "Give it" (or "Drop it") followed by "Good dog" and throwing it again. If he's reluctant to give it to you, offer a small treat so that he drops the toy as he takes the treat. He will soon get the idea.

completely reliable and steady with the down command. Again, don't rush it. With the dog in the down position on your left side, step out on your right foot as you say "Stay." Return by walking around in back of the dog and into your original position. While you are training, it's okay to murmur something like "Hold on" to encourage him to stay put. When the dog will stay without moving when you are at a distance of 3 or 4 feet, begin to increase the length of time before you return. Be sure he holds the down on your return until you say "Okay." At that point, he gets his treat—just so he'll remember for next time that it's not over until it's over.

THE COME EXERCISE

No command is more important to the safety of your English Cocker Spaniel than "Come." It is what you should say every single time you see the puppy running toward you: "Flush, come! Good dog."

During

TIPS FOR TRAINING AND SAFETY

1. Whether on- or off-leash, practice only in a fenced area.
2. Remove the training collar when the training session is over.
3. Don't try to break up a dogfight.
4. "Come," "Leave it" and "Wait" are safety commands.
5. The dog belongs in a crate or behind a barrier when riding in the car.
6. Don't ignore the dog's first sign of aggression. Aggression only gets worse, so take it seriously.
7. Keep the faces of children and dogs separated.
8. Pay attention to what the dog is chewing.
9. Keep the vet's number near your phone.
10. "Okay" is a useful release command.

playtime, run a few feet away from the puppy and turn and tell him to "Come" as he is already running to you. You can go so far as to teach your puppy two things at once if you squat down and hold out your arms. As the pup gets close to you and you're saying "Good dog," bring your right arm in about waist high. Now he's also learning the hand signal, an excellent device should you be on the phone when you need to get him to come to you! You'll also both be one step ahead when you enter obedience classes.

When the puppy responds to your well-timed "Come," try it with the puppy on the training leash. This time, catch him off guard, while he's sniffing a leaf or watching a bird: "Flush, come!" You may have to pause for a split second after his name to be sure you have his attention. If the puppy shows any sign of confusion, give the leash a mild jerk and take a couple of steps backward. Do not repeat the command. In this case, you should say "Good come" as he reaches you.

That's the number-one rule of training. Each command word is given just once. Anything more is nagging. You'll also notice that all commands are one word only. Even when they are actually two words, you say them as one.

Never call the dog to come to you—with or without his name—if you are angry or intend to correct him for some misbehavior. When correcting the pup, you go to him. Your dog must always connect "Come" with something pleasant and with your approval. He won't be eager to come to you if he anticipates being punished but will come reliably if he connects coming to you with something happy.

Puppies, like children, have notoriously short attention spans, so don't overdo it with any of the training. Keep each lesson short. Break it up with a quick run around the yard or a ball toss, repeat the lesson and quit as soon as the pup gets it right. That way, you will always end with a "Good dog."

Life isn't perfect and neither are puppies. A time will come, often around ten months of age, when he'll become "selectively deaf" or choose to "forget" his name. He may respond by wagging

Most successful show dogs are trained to the stand position by using food rewards as incentives.

his tail (and even seeming to smile at you) with a look that says "Make me!" Laugh, throw his favorite toy and skip the lesson you had planned.

THE HEEL EXERCISE
The second most important command to teach, after the come, is the heel. When you are walking your growing puppy, you need to be in control. Besides, it looks terrible to be pulled and yanked down the street, and it's not much fun either. Your eight-to ten-week-old puppy will probably follow you everywhere, but that's his natural instinct, not your control over the situation. However, any time he does follow you, you can say "Heel" and be ahead of the game, as he will learn to associate this command with the action of following you before you even begin teaching him to heel.

There is a very precise, almost military, procedure for teaching your dog to heel. As with all other obedience training, begin with the dog on your left side. He will be in a very nice sit and you will have the training leash across your chest. Hold the loop and folded leash in your right hand. Pick up the slack leash above the dog in your left hand and hold it loosely at your side. Step out on your left foot as you say "Heel." If the puppy does not move, give a gentle tug or pat your left leg to get him started. If he surges ahead of you, stop and pull him back gently until he is at your side. Tell him to sit and begin again.

Walk a few steps and stop while the puppy is correctly beside you. Tell him to sit and give mild verbal praise. (More enthusiastic praise will encourage him to think the lesson is over.) Repeat the lesson, increasing the number of steps you take only as long as the dog is heeling nicely beside you. When you end the lesson, have him hold the sit, then give him the "Okay" to let him know that this is the end of the lesson. Praise him so that he knows he did a good job.

The cure for excessive pulling (a common problem) is to stop when the dog is no more than 2 or 3 feet ahead of you. Guide him back into position and begin again. With a really determined puller, try switching to a head collar. This will automatically turn the pup's head toward you so you can bring

Training means more than just commands; it means enforcing the house rules as well. A mannerly English Cocker knows that your knitting is *not* for chewing.

him back easily to the heel position. Give quiet, reassuring praise every time the leash goes slack and he's staying with you.

Staying and heeling can take a lot out of a dog, so provide playtime and free-running exercise to shake off the stress when the lessons are over. You don't want him to associate training with all work and no fun.

TRAINING FOR THE FIELD
A spaniel's duties in the field consist of working close to the sportsman to quest for game, flush it and retrieve it when called upon to do so. If you want to train your English Cocker Spaniel for work, you have to start the pup at an early age. The basis for all training is obedience and that is where you

NO MORE TREATS!
When your dog is responding promptly and correctly to commands, it's time to eliminate treats. Begin by alternating a treat reward with a verbal-praise-only reward. Gradually eliminate all treats while increasing the frequency of praise. Overlook pleading eyes and expectant expressions, but if he's still watching your treat hand, you're on your way to using hand signals.

An English Cocker is usually an excellent retriever and swimmer. Introduce the pup to water slowly and test his skills in shallow waters. Once you are convinced of his ability to swim (choose safe bodies of water; be aware of currents), you can throw floatable toys into the water and train him to bring them to you. With a little encouragement, your English Cocker will swim out, retrieve the object and then bring it back to where you are waiting.

start with your puppy right away. Basic commands such as "Come," "Sit" and "Heel" can be taught to the puppy, and everything he learns under the age of six months old will not be forgotten. You can also start to teach him to retrieve a small object or dummy. This can be a sock or a rabbit skin or the wing of a bird. If you throw the object a few yards ahead of your puppy, he will run to it and pick it up. Call him by his name and encourage him to bring it back to you. Do not be discouraged if your puppy thinks this is a fun game and runs off with the object! If he does that, move away from him, calling him by his name. Always remember to reward him when he returns to you and whenever else possible.

The next lesson is to encourage him to use his nose. By dragging a piece of meat, you can make a trail for him to sniff out. You can also throw the dummy into light cover, where it is out of sight, and encourage your English Cocker to locate and then retrieve it. You must be very careful with the puppy when he starts teething because picking up the dummy might be quite painful for him and forcing him to pick it up would do irreparable harm to his willingness to retrieve. By the time your puppy is eight or nine months old, knows his basic obedience and has learned to retrieve and use his nose, you can join a field-training class. Depending on his natural aptitude, you may progress to training him for competition in hunting tests and field trials.

OTHER ACTIVITIES FOR LIFE

Whether a dog is trained in the structured environment of a class or alone with his owner at home, there are many activities that can bring fun and rewards to both owner and dog once they have mastered basic control.

Teaching the dog to help out around the home, in the yard or on the farm provides great satisfaction to both dog and owner. In addition, the dog's help makes life a little easier for his owner and raises his stature as a valued companion to his family. It helps give the dog a purpose; it helps to keep his mind occupied and provides an outlet for his energy.

Backpacking is an exciting and healthful activity that the dog can be taught without assistance from more than his owner. The exercise of walking and climbing is good

for man and dog alike, and the bond that they develop together is priceless.

If you are interested in participating in organized competition with your English Cocker, there are activities other than field and hunting events in which you and your dog can become involved. Competitive obedience builds on the basic commands and takes them to advanced levels. Agility is a popular and fun sport where dogs run through an obstacle course that includes various jumps, tunnels and other exercises to test the dog's speed and coordination. The owners run through the course beside their dogs to give commands and to guide them through the course. Although competitive, the focus is on fun— it's fun to do and fun to watch, as well as great exercise.

Illustrations from the late 1800s of the English Cocker Spaniel frequently depict the breed with retrieved game, indicating the breed's traditional use.

Eng. Ch. Colinwood Cowboy, a well-known English Cocker of the past, was a great pheasant retriever, as shown in this historic action photo.

HEALTHCARE OF YOUR

ENGLISH COCKER SPANIEL

By Lowell Ackerman, DVM, DACVD

HEALTHCARE FOR A LIFETIME

When you own a dog, you become his healthcare advocate over his entire lifespan, as well as being the one to shoulder the financial burden of such care. Accordingly, it is worthwhile to focus on prevention rather than treatment, as you and your pet will both be happier.

Of course, the best place to have begun your program of preventive healthcare is with the initial purchase or adoption of your dog. There is no way of guaranteeing that your new furry friend is free of medical problems, but there are some things you can do to improve your odds. You certainly should have done adequate research into the English Cocker Spaniel and have selected your puppy carefully rather than buying on impulse. Health issues aside, a large number of pet abandonment and relinquishment cases arise from a mismatch between pet needs and owner expectations. This is entirely preventable with appropriate planning and finding a good breeder.

Regarding healthcare issues specifically, it is very difficult to make blanket statements about where to acquire a problem-free pet, but, again, a reputable breeder is your best bet. In an ideal situation you have the opportunity to see both parents, get references from other owners of the breeder's pups and see genetic-testing documentation for several generations of the litter's ancestors. At the very least, you must thoroughly investigate your breed of interest and the problems inherent in that breed, as well as the genetic testing available to screen for those problems. Genetic testing offers some important benefits, but testing is available for only a few disorders in a relatively small number of breeds and is not available for some of the most common genetic diseases, such as hip dysplasia, cataracts, epilepsy, cardiomyopathy, etc. This area of research is indeed exciting and increasingly important, and advances will continue to be made each year. In fact, recent research has shown that there is an equivalent dog gene for 75% of known human genes, so research done in either species is likely to benefit the other.

We've also discussed that evaluating the behavioral nature of your English Cocker Spaniel and that of his immediate family members is an important part of the selection process that cannot be underestimated or overemphasized. It is sometimes difficult to evaluate temperament in puppies because certain behavioral tendencies, such as some forms of aggression, may not be immediately evident. More dogs are euthanized each year for behavioral reasons than for all medical conditions combined, so it is critical to take temperament issues seriously. Start with a well-balanced, friendly companion and put the time and effort into proper socialization, and you will both be rewarded with a lifelong valued relationship.

Assuming that you have started off with a pup from healthy, sound stock, you then become responsible for helping your veterinarian keep

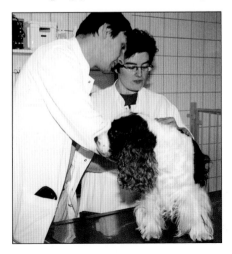

your pet healthy. Some crucial things happen before you even bring your puppy home. Parasite control typically begins at two weeks of age, and vaccinations typically begin at six to eight weeks of age. A pre-pubertal evaluation is typically scheduled for about six months of age. At this time, a dental evaluation is done (since the adult teeth are now in), heartworm prevention is started and neutering or spaying is most commonly done.

It is critical to commence regular dental care at home if you have not already done so. It may not sound very important, but most dogs have active periodontal disease by four years of age if they don't have their teeth cleaned regularly at home, not just at their veterinary exams. Dental problems lead to more than just bad "doggie breath." Gum disease can have very serious medical consequences. If you start brushing your dog's teeth and using antiseptic rinses from a young age, your dog will be accustomed to it and will not resist. The results will be healthy dentition, which your pet will need to enjoy a long, healthy life.

Most dogs are considered adults at a year of age, although some larger breeds still have some filling out to do up to about two or so years old. Even individual dogs within each breed have different healthcare requirements, so work with your veterinarian to determine what will be needed and what your

Select a reputable veterinarian close to your home and don't be hesitant to discuss fees, the equipment available, his office hours, emergency services and his experience with the breed.

ADAPTING TO AGE

As dogs age and their once-keen senses begin to deteriorate, they can experience stress and confusion. However, dogs are very adaptable, and most can adjust to deficiencies in their sight and hearing. As these processes often deteriorate gradually, the dog makes adjustments gradually, too. Because dogs become so familiar with the layout of their homes and yards, and with their daily routines, they are able to get around even if they cannot see or hear as well. Help your senior dog by keeping things consistent around the house. Keep up with your regular times for walking and potty trips, and do not relocate his crate or rearrange the furniture. Your dog is a very adaptable creature and can make compensation for his diminished ability, but you want to help him along the way and not make changes that will cause him confusion.

his anticipated lifespan, he is considered a "senior" and likely requires some special care. In general, if you've been taking great care of your canine companion throughout his formative and adult years, the transition to senior status should be a smooth one. Age is not a disease, and as long as everything is functioning as it should, there is no reason why most of late adulthood should not be rewarding for both you and your pet. This is especially true if you have tended to the details, such as regular veterinary visits, proper dental care, excellent nutrition and management of bone and joint issues.

At this stage in your English Cocker Spaniel's life, your veterinarian will likely want to schedule visits twice yearly, instead of once, to run some laboratory screenings, electrocardiograms and the like, and to change the diet to something more digestible. Catching problems early is the best way to manage them effectively. Treating the early stages of heart disease is so much easier than trying to intervene when there is more significant damage to the heart muscle. Similarly, managing the beginning of kidney problems is fairly routine if there is no significant kidney damage. Other problems, like cognitive dysfunction (similar to senility and Alzheimer's disease), cancer, diabetes and arthritis, are more common in older dogs, but all can be treated to help the dog live as

role should be. This doctor-client relationship is important, because as vaccination guidelines change, there may not be an annual "vaccine visit" scheduled. You must make sure that you see your veterinarian at least annually, even if no vaccines are due, because this is the best opportunity to coordinate healthcare activities and to make sure that no medical issues creep by unaddressed.

When your English Cocker Spaniel reaches three-quarters of

many happy, comfortable years as possible. Just as in people, medical management is more effective (and less expensive) when you catch things early.

SELECTING A VETERINARIAN

There is probably no more important decision that you will make regarding your pet's health-care than the selection of his doctor. Your pet's veterinarian will be a pediatrician, family-practice physician and gerontologist, depending on the dog's life stage, and will be the individual who makes recommendations regarding issues such as when specialists need to be consulted, when diagnostic testing and/or therapeutic intervention is needed and when you will need to seek outside emergency and critical-care services. Your vet will act as your advocate and liaison throughout these processes.

Everyone has his own idea about what to look for in a vet, an individual who will play a big role in his dog's (and, of course, his own) life for many years to come. For some, it is the compassionate caregiver with whom they hope to develop a professional relationship to span the lifetime of their dogs and even their future pets. For others, they are seeking a clinician with keen diagnostic and therapeutic insight who can deliver state-of-the-art healthcare. Still others need a veterinary facility that

is open evenings and weekends, is in close proximity or provides mobile veterinary services to accommodate their schedules; these people may not much mind that their dogs might see different veterinarians on each visit. Just as we have different reasons for selecting our own healthcare professionals

DENTAL WARNING SIGNS

A veterinary dental exam is necessary if you notice one or any combination of the following in your dog:
- Broken, loose or missing teeth
- Loss of appetite (which could be due to mouth pain or illness caused by infection)
- Gum abnormalities, including redness, swelling and bleeding
- Drooling, with or without blood
- Yellowing of the teeth or gumline, indicating tartar
- Bad breath

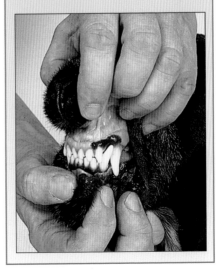

(e.g., covered by insurance plan, expert in field, convenient location, etc.), we should not expect that there is a one-size-fits-all recommendation for selecting a veterinarian and veterinary practice. The best advice is to be honest in your assessment of what you expect from a veterinary practice and to conscientiously research the options in your area. You will quickly appreciate that not all veterinary practices are the same, and you will be happiest with one that truly meets your needs.

There is another point to be considered in the selection of veterinary services. Not that long ago, a single veterinarian would attempt to manage all medical and surgical issues as they arose. That was often problematic, because veterinarians are trained in many species and many diseases, and it was just impossible for general veterinary practitioners to be experts in every species, every breed, every field and every ailment. However, just as in the human healthcare fields, specialization has allowed general practitioners to concentrate on primary healthcare delivery, especially wellness and the prevention of infectious diseases, and to utilize a network of specialists to assist in the management of conditions that require specific expertise and experience. Thus there are now many types of veterinary special-

YOUR DOG NEEDS TO VISIT THE VET IF:

- He has ingested a toxin such as antifreeze or a toxic plant; in these cases, administer first aid and call the vet right away
- His teeth are discolored, loose or missing or he has sores or other signs of infection or abnormality in the mouth
- He has been vomiting, has had diarrhea or has been constipated for over 24 hours; call immediately if you notice blood
- He has refused food for over 24 hours
- His eating habits, water intake or toilet habits have noticeably changed; if you have noticed weight gain or weight loss
- He shows symptoms of bloat, which requires *immediate* attention
- He is salivating excessively
- He has a lump in his throat
- He has a lump or bumps anywhere on the body
- He is very lethargic
- He appears to be in pain or otherwise has trouble chewing or swallowing
- His skin loses elasticity

Of course, there will be other instances in which a visit to the vet is necessary; these are just some of the signs that could be indicative of serious problems that need to be caught as early as possible.

ists, including dermatologists, cardiologists, ophthalmologists, surgeons, internists, oncologists,

TAKING YOUR DOG'S TEMPERATURE

It is important to know how to take your dog's temperature at times when you think he may be ill. It's not the most enjoyable task, but it can be done without too much difficulty. It's easier with a helper, preferably someone with whom the dog is friendly, so that one of you can hold the dog while the other inserts the thermometer.

Before inserting the thermometer, coat the end with petroleum jelly. Insert the thermometer slowly and gently into the dog's rectum about one inch. Wait for the reading, about two minutes. Be sure to remove the thermometer carefully and clean it thoroughly after each use.

A dog's normal body temperature is between 100.5 and 102.5 degrees F. Immediate veterinary attention is required if the dog's temperature is below 99 or above 104 degrees F.

advanced care and an unparalleled level of quality to be delivered.

With all of the opportunities for your English Cocker Spaniel to receive high-quality veterinary medical care, there is another topic that needs to be addressed at the same time—cost. It's been said that you can have excellent healthcare or inexpensive healthcare, but never both; this is as true in veterinary medicine as it is in human medicine. While veterinary costs are a fraction of what the same services cost in the human healthcare arena, it is still difficult to deal with unanticipated medical costs, especially since they can easily creep into hundreds or even thousands of dollars if specialists or emergency services become involved. However, there are ways of managing these risks. The easiest is to buy pet health insurance and realize that its foremost purpose is not to cover routine healthcare visits but rather to serve as an umbrella for those rainy days when

Liquid medicines can be given with a dropper-type tool to make it easier. Ask your veterinarian to demonstrate the best way to administer medication.

neurologists, behaviorists, criticalists and others to help primary-care veterinarians deal with complicated medical challenges. In most cases, specialists see cases referred by primary-care veterinarians, make diagnoses and set up management plans. From there, the animals' ongoing care is returned to their primary-care veterinarians. This important team approach to your pet's medical-care needs has provided opportunities for

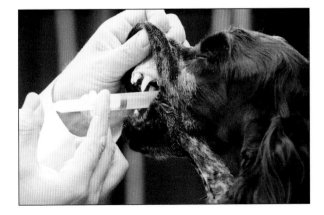

your pet needs medical care and you don't want to worry about whether or not you can afford it.

Pet insurance policies are very cost-effective (and very inexpensive by human health-insurance standards), but make sure that you buy the policy long before you intend to use it (preferably starting in puppyhood, because coverage will exclude pre-existing conditions) and that you are actually buying an indemnity insurance plan from an insurance company that is regulated by your state or province. Many insurance policy look-alikes are actually discount clubs that are redeemable only at specific locations and for specific services. An indemnity plan covers your pet at almost all veterinary, specialty and emergency practices and is an excellent way to manage your pet's ongoing health-care needs.

VACCINATIONS AND INFECTIOUS DISEASES

There has never been an easier time to prevent a variety of infectious diseases in your dog, but the advances we've made in veterinary medicine come with a price— choice. Now while it may seem that choice regarding vaccinations is a good thing, it also has never been more difficult for the pet owner (or the veterinarian) to make an informed decision about the best way to protect our pets through vaccination.

SIMULATED MEDICAL CONDITION FOR EDUCATIONAL PURPOSES ONLY.

HOT SPOTS

Patches of skin that become irritated and inflamed, referred to by veterinarians as acute moist dermatitis, are more commonly known as "hot spots." Abundantly coated breeds such as the English Cocker Spaniel are especially prone to these sores, which usually result from self-trauma. Some precipitating causes include otitis (inflammation of the ear), external parasites, anal sac irritation and other epidermal disorders that incite the dog to bite and/or scratch at the affected area. The incessant biting and scratching further irritate the skin, causing the superficial infection to become a moist weeping wound. Hot spots usually occur on the dog's hindquarters.

Years ago, it was just accepted that puppies got a starter series of vaccinations and then annual "boosters" throughout their lives to keep them protected. As more and more vaccines became available, consumers wanted the convenience of having all of that protection in a single injection. The result was "multivalent" vaccines that crammed a lot of protection into a single syringe. The manufacturers' recommendations were to give the vaccines annually, and this was a simple enough protocol to follow. However, as veterinary medicine has become more sophisticated and we have started looking more at healthcare quandaries rather than convenience, it became necessary to reevaluate the situation and deal with some tough questions. It is important to realize that whether or not to use a particular vaccine depends on the risk of contracting the disease against which it protects, the severity of the disease if it is contracted, the duration of immunity provided by the vaccine, the safety of the product and the needs of the individual animal. In a very general sense, rabies, distemper, hepatitis and parvovirus are considered core vaccine needs, while parainfluenza, *Bordetella bronchiseptica*, leptospirosis, coronavirus and borreliosis (Lyme disease) are considered non-core needs and best reserved for animals that demonstrate reasonable risk of contracting the diseases.

NEUTERING/SPAYING

Sterilization procedures (neutering for males/spaying for females) are meant to accomplish several purposes. While the underlying premise is to address the risk of pet overpopulation, there are also some medical and behavioral benefits to the surgeries as well. For females, spaying prior to the first estrus (heat cycle) leads to a marked reduction in the risk of mammary cancer and other serious female health problems. There also will be no manifestations of "heat" to attract male dogs and no bleeding in the house. For males, there is prevention of testicular cancer and a reduction in the risk of prostate problems. In both sexes there may be some limited reduction in aggressive behaviors toward other dogs, and some diminishing of urine marking, roaming and mounting.

While neutering and spaying do indeed prevent animals from contributing to pet overpopulation, even no-cost and low-cost neutering options have not eliminated the problem. Perhaps one of the main reasons for this is that individuals that intentionally breed their dogs and those that allow their animals to run at large are the main causes of unwanted offspring. Also, animals in shelters are often there because they were abandoned or relinquished, not because they came from unplanned matings. Neutering/spaying is important, but

Common Infectious Diseases

Let's discuss some of the diseases that create the need for vaccination in the first place. Following are the major canine infectious diseases and a simple explanation of each.

Rabies: A devastating viral disease that can be fatal in dogs and people. In fact, vaccination of dogs and cats is an important public-health measure to create a resistant animal buffer population to protect people from contracting the disease. Vaccination schedules are determined on a government level and are not optional for pet owners; rabies vaccination is required by law in all 50 states.

Parvovirus: A severe, potentially life-threatening disease that is easily transmitted between dogs. There are four strains of the virus, but it is believed that there is significant "cross-protection" between strains that may be included in individual vaccines.

Distemper: A potentially severe and life-threatening disease with a relatively high risk of exposure, especially in certain regions. In very high-risk distemper environments, young pups may be vaccinated with human measles vaccine, a related virus that offers cross-protection when administered at four to ten weeks of age.

Hepatitis: Caused by canine adenovirus type 1 (CAV-1), but since vaccination with the causative virus has a higher rate of adverse effects, cross-protection is derived from the use of adenovirus type 2 (CAV-2), a cause of respiratory disease and one of the potential causes of canine cough. Vaccination with CAV-2 provides long-term immunity against hepatitis, but relatively less protection against respiratory infection.

Canine cough: Also called tracheobronchitis, actually a fairly complicated result of viral and bacterial offenders; therefore, even with vaccination, protection is incomplete. Wherever dogs congregate, canine cough will likely be spread among them. Intranasal vaccination with *Bordetella* and parainfluenza is the best safeguard, but the duration of immunity does not appear to be very long, typically a year at most. These are non-core vaccines, but vaccination is sometimes mandated by boarding kennels, obedience classes, dog shows and other places where dogs congregate to try to minimize spread of infection.

Leptospirosis: A potentially fatal disease that is more common in some geographic regions. It is capable of being spread to humans. The disease varies with the individual "serovar," or strain, of *Leptospira* involved. Since there does not appear to be much cross-protection between serovars, protection is only as good as the likelihood that the serovar in the vaccine is the same as the one in the pet's local environment. Problems with *Leptospira* vaccines are that protection does not last very long, side effects are not uncommon and a large percentage of dogs (perhaps 30%) may not respond to vaccination.

Borrelia burgdorferi: The cause of Lyme disease, the risk of which varies with the geographic area in which the pet lives and travels. Lyme disease is spread by deer ticks in the eastern US and western black-legged ticks in the western part of the country, and the risk of exposure is high in some regions. Lameness, fever and inappetence are most commonly seen in affected dogs. The extent of protection from the vaccine has not been conclusively demonstrated.

Coronavirus: This disease has a high risk of exposure, especially in areas where dogs congregate, but it typically causes only mild to moderate digestive upset (diarrhea, vomiting, etc.). Vaccines are available, but the duration of protection is believed to be relatively short and the effectiveness of the vaccine in preventing infection is considered low.

There are many other vaccinations available, including those for *Giardia* and canine adenovirus-1. While there may be some specific indications for their use, and local risk factors to be considered, they are not widely recommended for most dogs.

it should be considered in the context of the real causes of animals' ending up in shelters and eventually being euthanized.

One of the important considerations regarding neutering is that it is a surgical procedure. This sometimes gets lost in discussions of low-cost procedures and commoditization of the process. In females, spaying is specifically referred to as an ovariohysterectomy. In this procedure, a midline incision is made in the abdomen and the entire uterus and both ovaries are surgically removed. While this is a major invasive surgical procedure, it usually has few complications, because it is typically performed on healthy young animals. However, it is major surgery, as any woman who has had a hysterectomy will attest.

In males, neutering has traditionally referred to castration, which involves the surgical removal of both testicles. While still a significant piece of surgery, there is not the abdominal exposure that is required in the female surgery. In addition, there is now a chemical sterilization option, in which a solution is injected into each testicle, leading to atrophy of the sperm-producing cells. This can typically be done under sedation rather than full anesthesia. This is a relatively new approach, and there are no long-term clinical studies yet available.

Neutering/spaying is typically done around six months of age at most veterinary hospitals, although techniques have been pioneered to perform the procedures in animals as young as eight weeks of age. In general, the surgeries on the very young animals are done for the specific reason of sterilizing them before they go to their new homes. This is done in some shelter hospitals for assurance that the animals will definitely not produce any pups. Otherwise, these organizations need to rely on owners to comply with their wishes to have the animals "altered" at a later date, something that does not always happen.

BREED-RELATED HEREDITARY CONDITIONS

FAMILIAL NEPHROPATHY (FN)

This is a very serious kidney disease in young English Cocker Spaniels that has been present in the breed for over 30 years. Signs of the disease are first seen from 12 weeks to two-and-a-half years of age. Once kidney failure begins, most pups fail to put on weight, then lose weight, start to become sick and eat less. Some show an increase in thirst and in urine output. A few develop diarrhea. Most pups then have less than two months before they become so ill that they have to be put down. There is no treatment available and the outcome is inevitable. FN is inherited as a simple recessive, which means that

---

THREADWORMS

Though less common than ascarids, hookworms and other nematodes, threadworms concern dog owners in the southwestern US and Gulf Coast area where the climate is hot and humid. Living in the small intestine of the dog, this worm measures a mere 2 millimeters and is round in shape. Like that of the whipworm, the threadworm's life cycle is very complex, and the eggs and larvae are passed through the feces. The cause of a deadly disease in humans, worms of the genus *Strongyloides* readily infect people; the handling of feces is the most common means of transmission. Threadworms are most often seen in young puppies; bloody diarrhea and pneumonia are symptoms. Sick puppies must be isolated and treated immediately; vets recommend a follow-up treatment one month later.

---

both parents must carry the gene to produce affected progeny. The ECSCA and the American Kennel Club are supporting research to find a genetic test for the disease.

HIP DYSPLASIA

This is a genetic problem whereby the acetabulum (hip socket) and the femoral head (top of thigh bone) do not fit together properly, causing pain and degeneration. It can only be diagnosed by scrutiny of an x-ray, which is done by specialists trained to do so.

The Orthopedic Foundation for Animals (OFA) has a testing scheme for hip dysplasia in which hip x-rays are submitted and evaluated by a panel of veterinarians. Dogs 24 months of age and older should have their hips x-rayed and the x-rays evaluated to determine if any degree of dysplasia is present. There are seven possible grades: Excellent, Good, Fair, Borderline, Mild, Moderate and Severe. Excellent,

Good and Fair are considered normal and dogs with these gradings will receive an OFA number. The other four gradings do not warrant an OFA number, with the latter three indicating that the dog is affected by some level of dysplasia. Dogs that do not receive OFA numbers should not be used in breeding programs.

When visiting a litter, a potential owner should ask to see documentation of the litter's parents' hip clearances from OFA or another accredited organization; similar hip-testing schemes are in place in countries around the world. Good breeders have all of their breeding stock tested and only breed from those dogs and bitches who have received appropriate clearances.

It is not a problem that affects English Cocker Spaniels very often, although the occurrence is slightly higher in solid-color than in parti-color Cockers. A low rate of occurrence does not mean that breeders should not be careful. Most breeders x-ray all of the dogs they use for breeding and eliminate those dogs with any degree of dysplasia from their breeding programs.

PROGRESSIVE RETINAL ATROPHY (PRA)

PRA is a congenital disease of the eye that is causing much concern in canine circles. It is inherited through a recessive gene, i.e., both parents must be carriers of the gene to produce afflicted offspring. The symptoms rarely manifest themselves until a dog is mature, sometimes even six or seven years of age, so that the dog or bitch may well have been used for breeding before the problem is detected. The disease can only be diagnosed by a specialist with special equipment. PRA is seen mostly in parti-color English Cocker Spaniels. The form of PRA seen in the breed is caused by the *prcd* (progressive rod-cone degeneration) gene, and a DNA marker test has been developed by OptiGen® with the hopes of eventually eradicating the disease from the breed.

CATARACTS

A cataract is a condition whereby the lens of the eyes will become covered with a milky film and the dog's eyesight will be seriously affected. It is often found in older dogs. However, cataracts can also be inherited and affect young English Cockers. Dogs that are being tested for PRA will normally also be tested for the presence of cataracts. Contrary to PRA, cataracts can occur in one eye only. The Canine Eye Registration Foundation (CERF) maintains a registry of dogs that have been tested for eye disease, as other hereditary eye problems can affect the breed as well.

ADDITIONAL HEREDITARY CONCERNS

While the main hereditary issues in the English Cocker are familial nephropathy, PRA-prcd and hip dysplasia, there are other problems not seen as often but to which breeders pay close attention and of which owners should be aware. Deafness can occur in parti-color English Cockers, as there seems to be a correlation between deafness and white coat color (as in Dalmatians, white Bull Terriers, etc.), although the inheritance is more complicated than just color-related. In the English Cocker deafness is present at birth and breeders are encouraged to utilize BAER (Brainstem Auditory Evoked Response) testing to detect deafness in their puppies. Epilepsy can be seen in all breeds; in the English Cocker, seizures are usually infrequent although some can be more severe. Epilepsy can be inherited but also can be brought on by other factors. Dilated cardiomyopathy is a heart condition that occurs mainly in solid English Cockers. Certain auto-immune diseases are found in the breed; for more information on these and other health issues in the English Cocker, visit the ECSCA's website: http://www.ecsca.org/healthcon.html

S. E. M. by Dr. Dennis Kunkel, University of Hawaii

A scanning electron micrograph of a dog flea, *Ctenocephalides canis*, on dog hair.

EXTERNAL PARASITES

FLEAS

Fleas have been around for millions of years and, while we have better tools now for controlling them than at any time in the past, there still is little chance that they will end up on an endangered species list. Actually, they are very well adapted to living on our pets, and they continue to adapt as we make advances.

The female flea can consume 15 times her weight in blood during active reproduction and can lay as many as 40 eggs a day. These eggs are very resistant to the effects of insecticides. They hatch into larvae, which then mature and spin cocoons. The immature fleas reside in this pupal stage until the time is right for feeding. This pupal stage is also very resistant to the effects of insecticides, and pupae can last in the environment without feeding for many months. Newly emergent fleas are attracted to animals by the warmth of the animals' bodies, movement and exhaled carbon dioxide. However, when they first emerge from their cocoons, they orient towards light; thus when an animal passes between a flea and the light source, casting a shadow, the flea pounces and starts to feed. If the animal turns out to be a dog or cat, the reproductive cycle continues. If the flea lands on another type of animal, including a person, the flea will bite but will then look for a more appropriate host. An emerging adult flea can survive without feeding for up to 12 months but, once it tastes blood, it can survive off its host for only three to four days.

It was once thought that fleas spend most of their lives in the environment, but we now know that fleas won't willingly jump off a dog unless leaping to another dog or when physically removed by brushing, bathing or other manipulation. Flea eggs, on the other hand, are shiny and smooth, and they roll off the animal and into the environment. The eggs, larvae and pupae then exist in the environment, but once the adult finds a susceptible animal, it's home sweet home until the flea is forced to seek refuge elsewhere.

Since adult fleas live on the animal and immature forms survive in the environment, a successful treatment plan must address all stages of the flea life cycle. There are now several safe and effective flea-control products that can be applied on a monthly

> ### FLEA PREVENTION FOR YOUR DOG
> - Discuss with your veterinarian the safest product to protect your dog, likely in the form of a monthly tablet or a liquid preparation placed on the back of the dog's neck.
> - For dogs suffering from flea-bite dermatitis, a shampoo or topical insecticide treatment is required.
> - Your lawn and property should be sprayed with an insecticide designed to kill fleas and ticks that lurk outdoors.
> - Using a flea comb, check the dog's coat regularly for any signs of parasites.
> - Practice good housekeeping. Vacuum floors, carpets and furniture regularly, especially in the areas that the dog frequents, and wash the dog's bedding weekly.
> - Follow up house-cleaning with carpet shampoos and sprays to rid the house of fleas at all stages of development. Insect growth regulators are the safest option.

basis. These include fipronil, imidacloprid, selamectin and permethrin (found in several formulations). Most of these products have significant flea-killing rates within 24 hours. However, none of them will control the immature forms in the environment. To accomplish this, there are a variety of insect growth regulators that can be

THE FLEA'S LIFE CYCLE

What came first, the flea or the egg? This age-old mystery is more difficult to comprehend than the actual cycle of the flea. Fleas usually live only about four months. A female can lay 2,000 eggs in her lifetime.

Egg

After ten days of rolling around your carpet or under your furniture, the eggs hatch into larvae, which feed on various and sundry debris. In days or

Larva

months, depending on the climate, the larvae spin cocoons and develop into the pupal or nymph stage, which quickly develop into fleas.

Pupa

These immature fleas must locate a host within 10 to 14 days or they will die. Only about 1% of the flea population exist as adult fleas, while the other 99% exist as eggs, larvae or pupae.

Adult

Photo by Carolina Biological Supply Co.

KILL FLEAS THE NATURAL WAY

If you choose not to go the route of conventional medication, there are some natural ways to ward off fleas:

- Dust your dog with a natural flea powder, composed of such herbal goodies as rosemary, wormwood, pennyroyal, citronella, rue, tobacco powder and eucalyptus.
- Apply diatomaceous earth, the fossilized remains of single-cell algae, to your carpets, furniture and pet's bedding. Even though it's not good for dogs, it's even worse for fleas, which will dry up swiftly and die.
- Brush your dog frequently, give him adequate exercise and let him fast occasionally. All of these activities strengthen the dog's system and make him more resistant to disease and parasites.
- Bathe your dog with a capful of pennyroyal or eucalyptus oil.
- Feed a natural diet, free of additives and preservatives. Add some fresh garlic and brewer's yeast to the dog's morning portion, as these items have flea-repelling properties.

sprayed into the environment (e.g., pyriproxyfen, methoprene, fenoxycarb) as well as insect development inhibitors such as lufenuron that can be administered. These compounds have no effect on adult fleas, but they stop immature forms from developing into adults. In years gone by, we relied heavily on toxic insecticides (such as organophosphates, organochlorines and carbamates) to manage the flea problem, but today's options are not only much safer to use on our pets but also safer for the environment.

TICKS

Ticks are members of the spider class (arachnids) and are blood-sucking parasites capable of transmitting a variety of diseases, including Lyme disease, ehrlichiosis, babesiosis and Rocky Mountain spotted fever. It's easy to see ticks on your own skin, but it is more of a challenge when your furry companion is affected. Whenever you happen to be planning a stroll in a tick-infested area (especially forests, grassy or wooded areas or parks) be prepared to do a thorough inspection of your dog afterward to search for ticks. Ticks can be tricky, so make sure you spend time looking in the ears, between the toes and everywhere else where a tick might hide. Ticks need to be attached for 24–72 hours before they transmit most of the diseases that they carry, so you do have a window of opportunity for some preventive intervention.

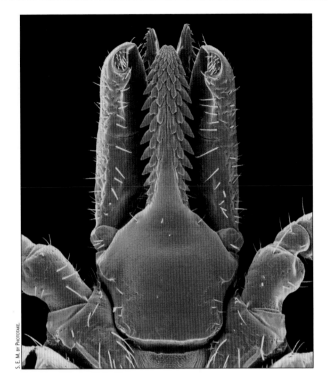

S. E. M. BY PHOTOTAKE.

A scanning electron micrograph of the head of a female deer tick, *Ixodes dammini*, a parasitic tick that carries Lyme disease.

A TICKING BOMB

There is nothing good about a tick's harpooning his nose into your dog's skin. Among the diseases caused by ticks are Rocky Mountain spotted fever, canine ehrlichiosis, canine babesiosis, canine hepatozoonosis and Lyme disease. If a dog is allergic to the saliva of a female wood tick, he can develop tick paralysis.

Female ticks live to eat and breed. They can lay between 4,000 and 5,000 eggs and they die soon after. Males, on the other hand, live only to mate with the females and continue the process as long as they are able. Most ticks live on multiple hosts before parasitizing dogs. The immature forms typically reside on grass and shrubs, waiting for suscep-tible animals to walk by. The larvae and nymph stages typically feed on wildlife.

If only a few ticks are present on a dog, they can be plucked out, but it is important to remove the entire head and mouthparts,

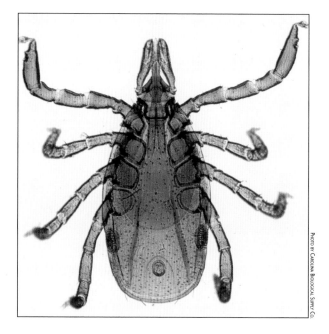

Photo by Carolina Biological Supply Co.

**Deer tick,
Ixodes dammini.**

disposed of in a container of alcohol or household bleach.

Some of the newer flea products, specifically those with fipronil, selamectin and permethrin, have effect against some, but not all, species of tick. Flea collars containing appropriate pesticides (e.g., propoxur, chlorfen-vinphos) can aid in tick control. In most areas, such collars should be placed on animals in March, at the beginning of the tick season, and changed regularly. Leaving the collar on when the pesticide level is waning invites the development of resistance. Amitraz collars are also good for tick control, and the active ingredient does not interfere with other flea-control products. The ingredient helps prevent the attachment of ticks to the skin and will cause those ticks already on the skin to detach themselves.

which may be deeply embedded in the skin. This is best accomplished with forceps designed especially for this purpose; fingers can be used but should be protected with rubber gloves, plastic wrap or at least a paper towel. The tick should be grasped as closely as possible to the animal's skin and should be pulled upward with steady, even pressure. Do not squeeze, crush or puncture the body of the tick or you risk exposure to any disease carried by that tick. Once the ticks have been removed, the sites of attachment should be disinfected. Your hands should then be washed with soap and water to further minimize risk of contagion. The tick should be

TICK CONTROL

Removal of underbrush and leaf litter and the thinning of trees in areas where tick control is desired are recom-mended. These actions remove the cover and food sources for small animals that serve as hosts for ticks. With continued mowing of grasses in these areas, the probability of ticks' surviving is further reduced. A variety of insecticide ingredients (e.g., resmethrin, carbaryl, permethrin, chlorpyrifos, dioxathion and allethrin) are registered for tick control around the home.

MITES

Mites are tiny arachnid parasites that parasitize the skin of dogs. Skin diseases caused by mites are referred to as "mange," and there are many different forms seen in dogs. These forms are very different from one another, each one warranting an individual description.

Sarcoptic mange, or scabies, is one of the itchiest conditions that affects dogs. The microscopic *Sarcoptes* mites burrow into the superficial layers of the skin and can drive dogs crazy with itchiness. They are also communicable to people, although they can't complete their reproductive cycle on people. In addition to being tiny, the mites also are often difficult to find when trying to make a diagnosis. Skin scrapings from multiple areas are examined microscopically but, even then, sometimes the mites cannot be found.

Fortunately, scabies is relatively easy to treat, and there are a variety of products that will successfully kill the mites. Since the mites can't live in the environment for very long without feeding, a complete cure is usually possible within four to eight weeks.

Cheyletiellosis is caused by a relatively large mite, which sometimes can be seen even without a microscope. Often referred to as "walking dandruff," this also causes itching, but not usually as profound as with scabies.

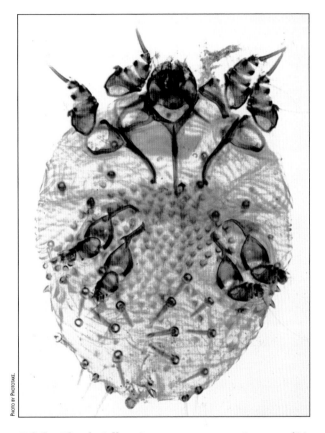

PHOTO BY PHOTOTAKE.

Sarcoptes scabiei, commonly known as the "itch mite."

While *Cheyletiella* mites can survive somewhat longer in the environment than scabies mites, they too are relatively easy to treat, being responsive to not only the medications used to treat scabies but also often to flea-control products.

Otodectes cynotis is the canine ear mite and is one of the more common causes of mange, especially in young dogs in shelters or pet stores. That's because the mites are typically present in large numbers and are quickly spread to

Micrograph of a dog louse, *Heterodoxus spiniger*. Female lice attach their eggs to the hairs of the dog. As the eggs hatch, the larval lice bite and feed on the blood. Lice can also feed on dead skin and hair. This feeding activity can cause hair loss and skin problems.

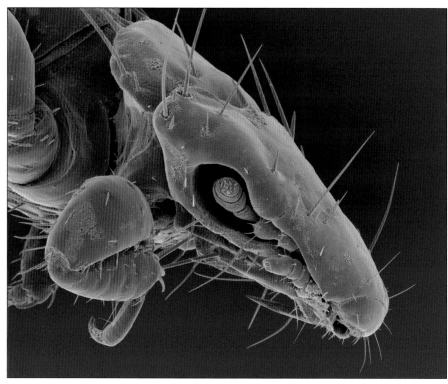

S. E. M. by Dr. Dennis Kunkel, University of Hawaii.

nearby animals. The mites rarely do much harm but can be difficult to eradicate if the treatment regimen is not comprehensive. While many try to treat the condition with ear drops only, this is the most common cause of treatment failure. Ear drops cause the mites to simply move out of the ears and as far away as possible (usually to the base of the tail) until the insecticide levels in the ears drop to an acceptable level—then it's back to business as usual! The successful treatment of ear mites requires treating all animals in the household with a systemic insecticide, such as selamectin, or a combination of miticidal ear drops combined with whole-body flea-control preparations.

Demodicosis, sometimes referred to as red mange, can be one of the most difficult forms of mange to treat. Part of the problem has to do with the fact that the mites live in the hair follicles and they are relatively well shielded from topical and systemic products. The main issue, however, is that demodectic mange typically results only when there is some underlying process interfering with the dog's immune system.

Since *Demodex* mites are

normal residents of the skin of mammals, including humans, there is usually a mite population explosion only when the immune system fails to keep the number of mites in check. In young animals, the immune deficit may be transient or may reflect an actual inherited immune problem. In older animals, demodicosis is usually seen only when there is another disease hampering the immune system, such as diabetes, cancer, thyroid problems or the use of immune-suppressing drugs. Accordingly, treatment involves not only trying to kill the mange mites but also discerning what is interfering with immune function and correcting it if possible.

Chiggers represent several different species of mite that don't parasitize dogs specifically, but do latch on to passersby and can cause irritation. The problem is most prevalent in wooded areas in the late summer and fall. Treatment is not difficult, as the mites do not complete their life cycle on dogs and are susceptible to a variety of miticidal products.

ILLUSTRATION BY PHOTOTAKE

Illustration of *Demodex folliculoram*.

MOSQUITOES

Mosquitoes have long been known to transmit a variety of diseases to people, as well as just being biting pests during warm weather. They also pose a real risk to pets. Not only do they carry deadly heartworms but recently there also has been much concern over their involvement with West Nile virus. While we can avoid heartworm with the use of preventive medications, there are no such preventives for West Nile virus. The only method of prevention in endemic areas is active mosquito control. Fortunately, most dogs that have been exposed to the virus only developed flu-like symptoms and, to date, there have not been the large number of reported deaths in canines as seen in some other species.

MOSQUITO REPELLENT

Low concentrations of DEET (less than 10%), found in many human mosquito repellents, have been safely used in dogs but, in these concentrations, probably give only about two hours of protection. DEET may be safe in these small concentrations, but since it is not licensed for use on dogs, there is no research proving its safety for dogs. Products containing permethrin give the longest-lasting protection, perhaps two to four weeks. As DEET is not licensed for use on dogs, and both DEET and permethrin can be quite toxic to cats, appropriate care should be exercised. Other products, such as those containing oil of citronella, also have some mosquito-repellent activity, but typically have a relatively short duration of action.

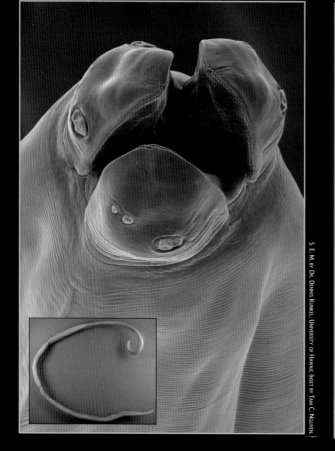

ASCARID DANGERS

The most commonly encountered worms in dogs are roundworms known as ascarids. *Toxascaris leonine* and *Toxocara canis* are the two species that infect dogs. Subsisting in the dog's stomach and intestines, adult roundworms can grow to 7 inches in length and adult females can lay in excess of 200,000 eggs in a single day.

In humans, visceral larval migrans affects people who have ingested eggs of *Toxocara canis*, which frequently contaminates children's sandboxes, beaches and park grounds. The roundworms reside in the human's stomach and intestines, as they would in a dog's, but do not mature. Instead, they find their way to the liver, lungs and skin, or even to the heart or kidneys in severe cases. Deworming puppies is critical in preventing the infection in humans, and young children should never handle nursing pups who have not been dewormed.

The ascarid roundworm *Toxocara canis,* showing the mouth with three lips. INSET: Photomicrograph of the roundworm *Ascaris lumbricoides.*

INTERNAL PARASITES: WORMS

ASCARIDS

Ascarids are intestinal roundworms that rarely cause severe disease in dogs. Nonetheless, they are of major public health significance because they can be transferred to people. Sadly, it is children who are most commonly affected by the parasite, probably from inadvertently ingesting ascarid-contaminated soil. In fact, many yards and children's sandboxes contain appreciable numbers of ascarid eggs. So, while ascarids don't bite dogs or latch onto their intestines to suck blood, they do cause some nasty medical conditions in children and are best eradicated from our furry friends. Because pups can start passing ascarid eggs by three weeks of age, most parasite-control programs begin at two weeks of age and are repeated every two weeks until pups are eight weeks old. It is important to

S. E. M. BY DR. DENNIS KUNKEL, UNIVERSITY OF HAWAII.

realize that bitches can pass ascarids to their pups even if they test negative prior to whelping. Accordingly, bitches are best treated at the same time as the pups.

HOOKWORMS

Unlike ascarids, hookworms do latch onto a dog's intestinal tract and can cause significant loss of blood and protein. Similar to ascarids, hookworms can be transmitted to humans, where they cause a condition known as cutaneous larval migrans. Dogs can become infected either by consuming the infective larvae or by the larvae's penetrating the skin directly. People most often get infected when they are lying on the ground (such as on a beach) and the larvae penetrate the skin. Yes, the larvae can penetrate through a beach blanket. Hookworms are typically susceptible to the same medications used to treat ascarids.

The hookworm *Ancylostoma caninum* infests the intestines of dogs. INSET: Note the row of hooks at the posterior end, used to anchor the worm to the intestinal wall.

WHIPWORMS

Whipworms latch onto the lower aspects of the dog's colon and can cause cramping and diarrhea. Eggs do not start to appear in the dog's feces until about three months after the dog was infected. This worm has a peculiar life cycle, which makes it more difficult to control than ascarids or hookworms. The good thing is that whipworms rarely are transferred to people.

Some of the medications used to treat ascarids and hookworms are also effective against whipworms, but, in general, a separate treatment protocol is needed. Since most of the medications are effective against the adults but not the eggs or larvae, treatment is typically repeated in three weeks, and then often in three

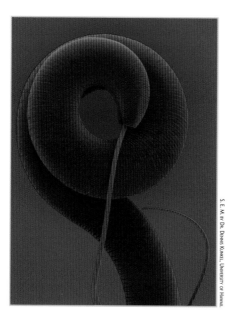

Adult whipworm, *Trichuris* sp., an intestinal parasite.

S. E. M. BY DR. DENNIS KUNKEL, UNIVERSITY OF HAWAII.

WORM-CONTROL GUIDELINES

- Practice sanitary habits with your dog and home.
- Clean up after your dog and don't let him sniff or eat other dogs' droppings.
- Control insects and fleas in the dog's environment. Fleas, lice, cockroaches, beetles, mice and rats can act as hosts for various worms.
- Prevent dogs from eating uncooked meat, raw poultry and dead animals.
- Keep dogs and children from playing in sand and soil.
- Kennel dogs on cement or gravel; avoid dirt runs.
- Administer heartworm preventives regularly.
- Have your vet examine your dog's stools at your annual visits.
- Select a boarding kennel carefully so as to avoid contamination from other dogs or an unsanitary environment.
- Prevent dogs from roaming. Obey local leash laws.

months as well. Unfortunately, since dogs don't develop resistance to whipworms, it is difficult to prevent them from getting reinfected if they visit soil contaminated with whipworm eggs.

TAPEWORMS

There are many different species of tapeworm that affect dogs, but *Dipylidium caninum* is probably the most common and is spread by fleas. Flea larvae feed on organic debris and tapeworm eggs in the environment and, when a dog chews at himself and manages to ingest fleas, he might get a dose of tapeworm at the same time. The tapeworm then develops further in the intestine of the dog.

The tapeworm itself, which is a parasitic flatworm that latches onto the intestinal wall, is composed of numerous segments. When the segments break off into the intestine (as proglottids), they may accumulate around the rectum, like grains of rice. While this tapeworm is disgusting in its behavior, it is not directly communicable to humans (although humans can also get infected by swallowing fleas).

A much more dangerous flatworm is *Echinococcus multiloc-ularis*, which is typically found in foxes, coyotes and wolves. The eggs are passed in the feces and infect rodents, and, when dogs eat the rodents, the dogs can be infected by thousands of adult tapeworms. While the parasites don't cause many problems in dogs, this is considered the most lethal worm infection that people can get. Take appropriate precautions if you live in an area in which these tapeworms are found. Do not use mulch that may contain feces of dogs, cats or wildlife, and

discourage your pets from hunting wildlife. Treat these tapeworm infections aggressively in pets, because if humans get infected, approximately half die.

HEARTWORMS

Heartworm disease is caused by the parasite *Dirofilaria immitis* and is seen in dogs around the world. A member of the roundworm group, it is spread between dogs by the bite of an infected mosquito. The mosquito injects infective larvae into the dog's skin with its bite, and these larvae develop under the skin for a period of time before making their way to the heart. There they develop into adults, which grow and create blockages of the heart, lungs and major blood vessels there. They also start producing offspring (microfilariae)

A dog tapeworm proglottid (body segment).

The dog tapeworm *Taenia pisiformis*.

S. E. M. BY DR. DENNIS KUNKEL, UNIVERSITY OF HAWAII.

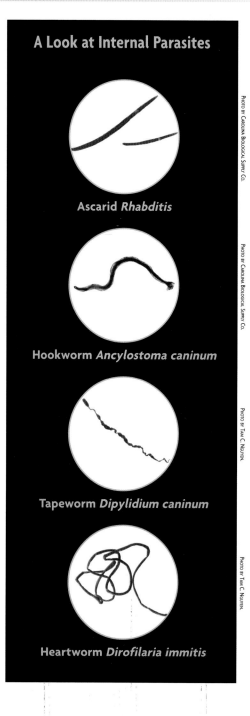

A Look at Internal Parasites

Ascarid *Rhabditis*

PHOTO BY CAROLINA BIOLOGICAL SUPPLY CO.

Hookworm *Ancylostoma caninum*

PHOTO BY CAROLINA BIOLOGICAL SUPPLY CO.

Tapeworm *Dipylidium caninum*

PHOTO BY TAM C. NGUYEN.

Heartworm *Dirofilaria immitis*

PHOTO BY TAM C. NGUYEN.

and these microfilariae circulate in the bloodstream, waiting to hitch a ride when the next mosquito bites. Once in the mosquito, the microfilariae develop into infective larvae and the entire process is repeated.

When dogs get infected with heartworm, over time they tend to develop symptoms associated with heart disease, such as coughing, exercise intolerance and potentially many other manifestations. Diagnosis is confirmed by either seeing the microfilariae themselves in blood samples or using immunologic tests (antigen testing) to identify the presence of adult heartworms. Since antigen tests measure the presence of adult heartworms and microfilarial tests measure offspring produced by adults, neither are positive until six to seven months after the initial infection. However, the beginning of damage can occur by fifth-stage larvae as early as three months after infection. Thus it is possible for dogs to be harboring problem-causing larvae for up to three months before either type of test would identify an infection.

The good news is that there are great protocols available for preventing heartworm in dogs. Testing is critical in the process, and it is important to understand the benefits as well as the limitations of such testing. All dogs six months of age or older that have not been on continuous heartworm-preventive medication should be

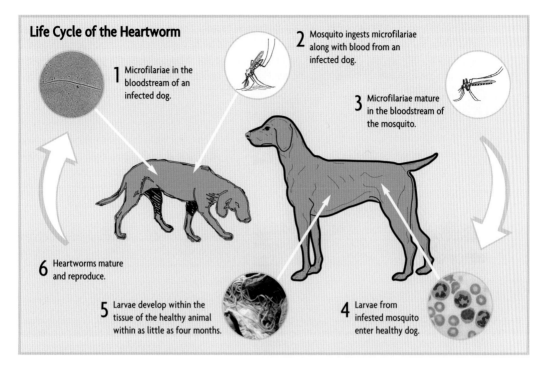

Life Cycle of the Heartworm

1 Microfilariae in the bloodstream of an infected dog.

2 Mosquito ingests microfilariae along with blood from an infected dog.

3 Microfilariae mature in the bloodstream of the mosquito.

4 Larvae from infested mosquito enter healthy dog.

5 Larvae develop within the tissue of the healthy animal within as little as four months.

6 Heartworms mature and reproduce.

screened with microfilarial or antigen tests. For dogs receiving preventive medication, periodic antigen testing helps assess the effectiveness of the preventives. The American Heartworm Society guidelines suggest that annual retesting may not be necessary when owners have absolutely provided continuous heartworm prevention. Retesting on a two- to three-year interval may be sufficient in these cases. However, your veterinarian will likely have specific guidelines under which heartworm preventives will be prescribed, and many prefer to err on the side of safety and retest annually.

It is indeed fortunate that heartworm is relatively easy to prevent, because treatments can be as life-threatening as the disease itself. Treatment requires a two-step process that kills the adult heartworms first and then the microfilariae. Prevention is obviously preferable; this involves a once-monthly oral or topical treatment. The most common oral preventives include ivermectin (not suitable for some breeds), moxidectin and milbemycin oxime; the once-a-month topical drug selamectin provides heartworm protection in addition to flea, tick and other parasite controls.

THE **ABC**s OF
Emergency Care

Abrasions
Clean wound with running water or 3% hydrogen peroxide. Pat dry with gauze and spray with antibiotic. Do not cover.

Animal Bites
Clean area with soap and saline solution or water. Apply pressure to any bleeding area. Apply antibiotic ointment. Identify animal and contact the vet.

Antifreeze Poisoning
Induce vomiting and take dog to the vet.

Bee Sting
Remove stinger and apply soothing lotion or cold compress; give antihistamine in proper dosage.

Bleeding
Apply pressure directly to wound with gauze or towel for five to ten minutes. If wound does not stop bleeding, wrap wound with gauze and adhesive tape.

Bloat/Gastric Torsion
Immediately take the dog to the vet or emergency clinic; phone from car. No time to waste.

Burns
Chemical: Bathe dog with water and pet shampoo. Rinse in saline solution. Apply antibiotic ointment.

Acid: Rinse with water. Apply one part baking soda, two parts water to affected area.

Alkali: Rinse with water. Apply one part vinegar, four parts water to affected area.

Electrical: Apply antibiotic ointment. Seek veterinary assistance immediately.

Choking
If the dog is on the verge of collapsing, wedge a solid object, such as the handle of a screwdriver, between molars on one side of mouth to keep mouth open. Pull tongue out. Use long-nosed pliers or fingers to remove foreign object. Do not push the object down the dog's throat. For small or medium dogs, hold dog upside down by hind legs and shake firmly to dislodge foreign object.

Chlorine Ingestion
With clean water, rinse the mouth and eyes. Give dog water to drink; contact the vet.

Constipation
Feed dog 2 tablespoons bran flakes with each meal. Encourage drinking water. Mix 1/4 teaspoon mineral oil in dog's food.

Diarrhea
Withhold food for 12 to 24 hours. Feed dog antidiarrheal with eyedropper. When feeding resumes, feed one part boiled hamburger, one part plain cooked rice, 1/4 to 3/4 cup four times daily.

Dog Bite
Snip away hair around puncture wound; clean with 3% hydrogen peroxide; apply tincture of iodine. If wound appears deep, take the dog to the vet.

Frostbite
Wrap the dog in a heavy blanket. Warm affected area with a warm bath for ten minutes. Red color to skin will return with circulation; if tissues are pale after 20 minutes, contact the vet.

Use a portable, durable container large enough to contain all items.

DOG OWNER'S FIRST-AID KIT

- ❑ **Gauze bandages/swabs**
- ❑ **Adhesive and non-adhesive bandages**
- ❑ **Antibiotic powder**
- ❑ **Antiseptic wash**
- ❑ **Hydrogen peroxide 3%**
- ❑ **Antibiotic ointment**
- ❑ **Lubricating jelly**
- ❑ **Rectal thermometer**
- ❑ **Nylon muzzle**
- ❑ **Scissors and forceps**
- ❑ **Eyedropper**
- ❑ **Syringe**
- ❑ **Anti-bacterial/fungal solution**
- ❑ **Saline solution**
- ❑ **Antihistamine**
- ❑ **Cotton balls**
- ❑ **Nail clippers**
- ❑ **Screwdriver/pen knife**
- ❑ **Flashlight**
- ❑ **Emergency phone numbers**

Heat Stroke
Partially submerge the dog in cold water; if no response within ten minutes, contact the vet.

Hot Spots
Mix 2 packets Domeboro® with 2 cups water. Saturate cloth with mixture and apply to hot spots for 15 to 30 minutes. Apply antibiotic ointment. Repeat every six to eight hours.

Poisonous Plants
Wash affected area with soap and water. Cleanse with alcohol. For foxtail/grass, apply antibiotic ointment. Contact the vet if plant is ingested.

Rat Poison Ingestion
Induce vomiting. Keep dog calm, maintain dog's normal body temperature (use blanket or heating pad). Get to the vet for antidote.

Shock
Keep the dog calm and warm; call for veterinary assistance.

Snake Bite
If possible, bandage the area and apply pressure. If the area is not conducive to bandaging, use ice to control bleeding. Get immediate help from the vet.

Tick Removal
Apply flea and tick spray directly on tick. Wait one minute. Using tweezers or wearing plastic gloves, apply constant pull while grasping tick's body. Apply antibiotic ointment.

Vomiting
Restrict dog's water intake; offer a few ice cubes. Withhold food for next meal. Contact vet if vomiting persists longer than 24 hours.

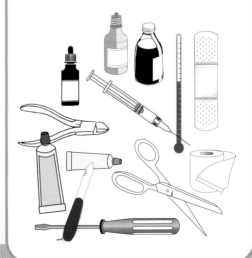

CANINE COGNITIVE DYSFUNCTION

"OLD-DOG" SYNDROME

There are many ways for you to evaluate old-dog syndrome. Veterinarians have defined canine cognitive dysfunction as the gradual deterioration of cognitive abilities, indicated by changes in the dog's behavior. When a dog changes his routine response, and maladies have been eliminated as the cause of these behavioral changes, then canine cognitive dysfunction is the usual diagnosis.

More than half the dogs over eight years old suffer from some form of this syndrome. The older the dog, the more chance he has of suffering from it. In humans, doctors often dismiss the canine cognitive dysfunction behavioral changes as part of "winding down."

There are four major signs of canine cognitive dysfunction: frequent potty accidents inside the home, sleeping much more or much less than normal, acting confused and failing to respond to social stimuli.

SYMPTOMS

FREQUENT POTTY ACCIDENTS
- Urinates in the house.
- Defecates in the house.
- Doesn't signal that he wants to go out.

FAILURE TO RESPOND TO SOCIAL STIMULI
- Comes to people less frequently, whether called or not.
- Doesn't tolerate petting for more than a short time.
- Doesn't come to the door when you return home.

CONFUSION
- Goes outside and just stands there.
- Appears confused with a faraway look in his eyes.
- Hides more often.
- Doesn't recognize friends.
- Doesn't come when called.
- Walks around listlessly and without a destination.

SLEEP PATTERNS
- Awakens more slowly.
- Sleeps more than normal during the day.
- Sleeps less during the night.

Number-One Killer Disease in Dogs: CANCER

In every age, there is a word associated with a disease or plague that causes humans to shudder. In the 21st century, that word is "cancer." Just as cancer is the leading cause of death in humans, it claims nearly half the lives of dogs that die from a natural disease as well as half the dogs that die over the age of ten years.

Described as a genetic disease, cancer becomes a greater risk as the dog ages. Vets and dog owners have become increasingly aware of the threat of cancer to dogs. Statistics reveal that one dog in every five will develop cancer, the most common of which is skin cancer. Many cancers, including prostate, ovarian and breast cancer, can be avoided by spaying and neutering our dogs by the age of six months.

Early detection of cancer can save or extend a dog's life, so it is absolutely vital for owners to have their dogs examined by a qualified vet or oncologist immediately upon detection of any abnormality. Certain dietary guidelines have also proven to reduce the onset and spread of cancer. Foods based on fish rather than beef, due to the presence of Omega-3 fatty acids, are recommended. Other amino acids such as glutamine have significant benefits for canines, particularly those breeds that show a greater susceptibility to cancer.

Cancer management and treatments promise hope for future generations of canines. Since the disease is genetic, breeders should never breed a dog whose parents, grandparents and any related siblings have developed cancer. It is difficult to know whether to exclude an otherwise healthy dog from a breeding program, as the disease does not manifest itself until the dog's senior years.

RECOGNIZE CANCER WARNING SIGNS

Since early detection can possibly rescue your dog from becoming a cancer statistic, it is essential for owners to recognize the possible signs and seek the assistance of a qualified professional.

- Abnormal bumps or lumps that continue to grow
- Bleeding or discharge from any body cavity
- Persistent stiffness or lameness
- Recurrent sores or sores that do not heal
- Inappetence
- Breathing difficulties
- Weight loss
- Bad breath or odors
- General malaise and fatigue
- Eating and swallowing problems
- Difficulty urinating and defecating

The Ten Most Common Fatal Diseases in Pure-bred Dogs

Disease	Percentage
Cancer	47%
Heart disease	12%
Kidney disease	7%
Epilepsy	4%
Liver disease	4%
Bloat	3%
Diabetes	3%
Stroke	2%
Cushing's disease	2%
Immune diseases	2%
Other causes	14%

ENGLISH COCKER SPANIEL

DO YOU WANT TO SHOW?

Is dog showing in your blood? Are you excited by the idea of gaiting your handsome English Cocker Spaniel around the ring to the thunderous applause of an enthusiastic audience? Are you certain that your beloved English Cocker Spaniel is flawless? You are not alone! Every loving owner thinks that his dog has no faults, or too few to mention. No matter how many times an owner reads the breed standard, he cannot find any faults in his aristocratic companion dog. If this sounds like you, and if you are considering entering your English Cocker Spaniel in a dog show, here are some basic questions to ask yourself:

- Did you purchase a "show-quality" puppy from the breeder?
- Is your puppy at least six months of age?
- Does the puppy exhibit correct show type for his breed?
- Does your puppy have any disqualifying faults?
- Is your English Cocker Spaniel registered with the American Kennel Club?
- How much time do you have to devote to training, grooming,

FIVE CLASSES AT SHOWS

At most AKC all-breed shows, there are five regular classes offered: Puppy, Novice, Bred-by-Exhibitor, American-bred and Open. The Puppy Class is usually divided as 6 to 9 months of age and 9 to 12 months of age. When deciding in which class to enter your dog, whether male or female, you must carefully check the show schedule to make sure that you have selected the right class. Depending on the age of the dog, previous first-place wins and the sex of the dog, you must make the best choice. It is possible to enter a one-year-old dog who has not won sufficient first places in any of the non-Puppy Classes, though the competition is more intense the further you progress from the Puppy Class.

Learning to pose your English Cocker to display his best attributes is half of the battle of showing. Clever handling, however, will not fool an eagle-eyed judge.

AKC GROUPS

For showing purposes, the American Kennel Club divides its recognized breeds into seven groups: Sporting Dogs, Hounds, Working Dogs, Terriers, Toys, Non-Sporting Dogs and Herding Dogs.

It just doesn't get any better than Best in Show at Crufts. Following the tradition of famous English Cockers of yesteryear, here's Eng. Sh. Ch. Caniou Cambrai, reigning as the show's Champion of Champions.

conditioning and exhibiting your dog?
- Do you understand the rules and regulations of a dog show?
- Do you have time to learn how to show your dog properly?
- Do you have the financial resources to invest in showing your dog?
- Will you show the dog yourself or hire a professional handler?
- Do you have a vehicle that can accommodate your weekend trips to the dog shows?

Success in the show ring requires more than a pretty face,

An English Cocker Spaniel competing at a local show in the Netherlands. There are many lovely English Cockers bred on the Continent, and they are always popular at shows.

English, Dutch and German Champion Speggle-Waggel's Quible was a top English Cocker Spaniel bitch in the Netherlands.

a waggy tail and a pocketful of liver. Even though dog shows can be exciting and enjoyable, the sport of conformation makes great demands on the exhibitors and the dogs. Winning exhibitors live for their dogs, devoting time and money to their dogs' presentation, conditioning and training. Very few novices, even those with good dogs, will find themselves in the winners'

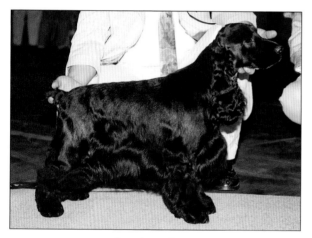

Eng. Sh. Ch. Quettadene Make Believe lives in Hungary and became an International champion.

circle, though it does happen. Don't be disheartened, though. Every exhibitor began as a novice and worked his way up to the Group ring. It's the "working your way up" part that you must keep in mind.

Assuming that you have purchased a puppy of the correct type and quality for showing, let's begin to examine the world of showing and what's required to get started. Although the entry fee into a dog show is nominal,

there are lots of other hidden costs involved with "finishing" your English Cocker Spaniel, that is, making him a champion. Things like equipment, travel, training and conditioning all cost money. A more serious campaign will include fees for a professional handler, boarding, cross-country travel and advertising. Top-winning show dogs can

BECOMING A CHAMPION

An official AKC championship of record requires that a dog accumulate 15 points under three different judges, including two "majors" under different judges. Points are awarded based on the number of dogs entered into competition, varying from breed to breed and place to place. A win of three, four or five points is considered a "major." The AKC annually assigns a schedule of points to adjust to the variations that accompany a breed's popularity and the population of a given area.

represent a very considerable investment—over $100,000 has been spent in campaigning some dogs. (The investment can be less, of course, for owners who don't use professional handlers.)

Many owners, on the other hand, enter their "average" English Cocker Spaniels in dog shows for the fun and enjoyment of it. Dog showing makes an absorbing hobby, with many rewards for dogs and owners alike. If you're having fun, meeting other people who share your interests and enjoying the overall experience, you likely will catch the "bug." Once the dog-show bug bites, its effects can last a lifetime; it's certainly

The judge thoroughly examines the English Cocker Spaniel on the table. The handler's job is to keep the dog calm but alert and looking his best as he accepts the judge's examination.

much better than a deer tick! Soon you will be envisioning yourself in the center ring at the Westminster Kennel Club Dog Show in New York City, competing for the prestigious Best in Show cup. This magical dog show is televised annually from Madison Square Garden, and the victorious dog becomes a celebrity overnight.

AKC CONFORMATION BASICS
Visiting a dog show as a spectator is a great place to start. Pick up the show catalog to find out what time your breed is being shown, who is judging the breed and in which ring the classes will be held. To start, English Cocker Spaniels compete against other English Cocker Spaniels, and the winner is selected as Best of Breed by the judge. This is the procedure for each breed. At a group show, all of the Best of Breed winners go

---

DRESS THE PART
It's a dog show, so don't forget *your* "costume." Even though the show is about the dog, you also must play your role well. You have been cast as the "dog handler" and you must smartly dress the part. Solid colors make a nice complement to the dog's coat, but choose colors that contrast. You don't want to be wearing a solid color that blends mostly or entirely with the major or only color of your dog. Whether the show is indoors or out, you still must dress properly. You want the judge to perceive you as being professional, so polish, polish, polish! And don't forget to wear sensible shoes; remember, you have to gait around the ring with your dog.

Here's Eng. Sh. Ch. Caniou Cambrai with Mrs. P. Bentley. This photo captures a happy moment between dog and handler immediately following the announcement that they had won Best in Show at Crufts in 1996.

on to compete for Group One in their respective groups. For example, all Best of Breed winners in a given group compete against each other; this is done for all seven groups. Finally, all seven group winners go head to head in the ring for the Best in Show award.

What most spectators don't understand is the basic idea of conformation. A dog show is often referred as a "conformation" show. This means that the judge should decide how each dog stacks up (conforms) to the breed standard for his given breed: how well does this English Cocker Spaniel conform to the ideal representative detailed in the standard? Ideally, this is what happens. In reality, however, this ideal often gets slighted as the judge compares English Cocker Spaniel #1 to English Cocker Spaniel #2. Again, the ideal is that each dog is judged based on his merits in comparison to his breed standard, not in comparison to the other dogs in the ring. It is easier for judges to compare dogs of the same breed to decide which they think is the better specimen; in the Group and Best in Show ring, however, it is very difficult to compare one breed to another, like apples to oranges. Thus the dog's conformation to the breed standard—not to mention advertising dollars and good handling—is essential to success in conformation shows. The dog described in the standard (the standard for each AKC breed is written and approved by the breed's national parent club and then submitted to the AKC for approval) is the perfect dog of that breed, and breeders keep their eye on the standard when they choose which dogs to breed, hoping to get closer and closer to the ideal with each litter.

Another good first step for the novice is to join a dog club.

You will be astonished by the many and different kinds of dog clubs in the country, with about 5,000 clubs holding events every year. Most clubs require that prospective new members present two letters of recommendation from existing members. Perhaps you've made some friends visiting a show held by a particular club and you would like to join that club. Dog clubs may specialize in a single breed, like a local or regional English Cocker Spaniel club, or in a specific pursuit, such as obedience, tracking or hunting tests. There are all-breed clubs for all dog enthusiasts; they often sponsor special training days, seminars on topics like grooming or handling or lectures on breeding or canine genetics. There are also clubs that specialize in certain types of dogs, like spaniel breeds, hunting dogs, companion dogs, etc.

A parent club is the national organization, sanctioned by the AKC, which promotes and safeguards its breed in the country. The English Cocker Spaniel Club of America was formed in 1936 and can be contacted on the Internet at www.ecsca.org. The parent club holds an annual national specialty show, usually in a different city each year, in which many of the country's top dogs,

This puppy looked very promising at seven weeks of age...

At seven months of age, the youngster is filling out and looking even better...

At two years of age, the dog became a full-fledged champion, having won championships in Holland, Germany and Monaco...

The dog is known as Ch. Speggle-Waggel's Haighla.

handlers and breeders gather to compete. At a specialty show, only members of a single breed are invited to participate. There are also group specialties, in which all members of a group are invited. For more information about dog clubs in your area, contact the AKC at www.akc.org on the Internet or write them at their Raleigh, NC address.

OTHER TYPES OF COMPETITION

In addition to conformation shows, the AKC holds a variety of other competitive events. Obedience trials, agility trials and tracking trials are open to all breeds, while hunting tests, field trials, lure coursing, herding tests and trials, earthdog tests and coonhound events are limited to specific breeds or groups of breeds. The Junior Showmanship program is offered to aspiring young handlers and their dogs, and the Canine Good Citizen® program is an all-around good-behavior test open to all dogs, pure-bred and mixed.

OBEDIENCE TRIALS

Mrs. Helen Whitehouse Walker, a Standard Poodle fancier, can be credited with introducing obedience trials to the United States. In the 1930s she designed a series of exercises based on those of the Associated Sheep,

Police, Army Dog Society of Great Britain. These exercises were intended to evaluate the working relationship between dog and owner. Since those early days of the sport in the US, obedience trials have grown more and more popular, and now more than 2,000 trials each year attract over 100,000 dogs and their owners. Any dog registered with the AKC, regardless of neutering or other disqualifications that would preclude entry in conformation competition, can participate in obedience trials.

There are three levels of

FOR MORE INFORMATION...

For reliable up-to-date information about registration, dog shows and other canine competitions, contact one of the national registries by mail or via the Internet:

American Kennel Club
5580 Centerview Dr., Raleigh, NC 27606-3390
www.akc.org

United Kennel Club
100 E. Kilgore Road, Kalamazoo, MI 49002
www.ukcdogs.com

Canadian Kennel Club
89 Skyway Ave., Suite 100, Etobicoke, Ontario
M9W 6R4, Canada
www.ckc.ca

The Kennel Club
1-5 Clarges St., Piccadilly, London W1Y 8AB, UK
www.the-kennel-club.org.uk

Winning in the conformation ring brings prestige to the English Cocker owner. The breed can add further distinction to a championship title by winning in field events.

difficulty in obedience competition. The first (and easiest) level is the Novice, in which dogs can earn the Companion Dog (CD) title. The intermediate level is the Open level, in which the Companion Dog Excellent (CDX) title is awarded. The advanced level is the Utility level, in which dogs compete for the Utility Dog (UD) title. Classes at each level are further divided into "A" and "B," with "A" for beginners and "B" for those with more experience. In order to win a title at a given level, a dog must earn three "legs." A "leg" is accomplished when a dog scores 170 or higher (200 is a perfect score). The scoring system gets a little trickier when

you understand that a dog must score more than 50% of the points available for each exercise in order to actually earn the points. Available points for each exercise range between 20 and 40.

Once he's earned the UD title, a dog can go on to win the prestigious title of Utility Dog Excellent (UDX) by winning "legs" in ten shows. Additionally, Utility Dogs who win "legs" in Open B and Utility B earn points toward the lofty title of Obedience Trial Champion (OTCh.). Established in 1977 by the AKC, this title requires a dog to earn 100 points as well as three first places in a combination of Open B and Utility B classes under three different judges. The "brass ring" of obedience competition is the AKC's National Obedience Invitational. This is an exclusive competition for only the cream of the obedience crop. In order to qualify for the invitational, a dog must be ranked in either the top 25 all-breeds in obedience or in the top three for his breed in obedience. The title at stake here is that of National Obedience Champion (NOC).

AGILITY TRIALS

Agility trials became sanctioned by the AKC in August 1994, when the first licensed agility trials were held. Since that time, agility certainly has grown in popularity by leaps and bounds, literally! The AKC allows all registered breeds (including Miscellaneous Class breeds) to participate, providing the dog is 12 months of age or older. Agility is designed so that the handler demonstrates how well the dog can work at his side. The handler directs his dog through, over, under and around an obstacle course that includes jumps, tires, the dog walk, weave poles, pipe tunnels, collapsed tunnels and more. While working his way through the course, the dog must keep one eye and ear on the handler and the rest of his body on the course. The handler runs along with the dog, giving verbal and hand signals to guide the dog through the course.

The first organization to

TRACKING

Tracking tests are exciting ways to test your English Cocker Spaniel's instinctive scenting ability on a competitive level. All dogs have a nose, and all breeds are welcome in tracking tests. The first AKC-licensed tracking test took place in 1937 as part of the Utility level at an obedience trial, and thus competitive tracking was officially begun. The first title, Tracking Dog (TD), was offered in 1947, ten years after the first official tracking test. It was not until 1980 that the AKC added the title Tracking Dog Excellent (TDX), which was followed by the title Versatile Surface Tracking (VST) in 1995. Champion Tracker (CT) is awarded to a dog who has earned all three of those titles.

The TD level is the first and most basic level in tracking, progressing in difficulty to the TDX and then the VST. A dog must follow a track laid by a human 30 to 120 minutes prior in order to earn the TD title. The track is about 500 yards long and contains up to 5 directional changes. At the next level, the TDX, the dog must follow a 3- to 5-hour-old track over a course that is up to 1,000 yards long and has up to 7 directional changes. In the most difficult level, the VST, the track is up to 5 hours old and located in an urban setting.

A Best in Show win is a truly unforgettable moment for a dog and handler who have worked so hard together to achieve this goal.

promote agility trials in the US was the United States Dog Agility Association, Inc. (USDAA). Established in 1986, the USDAA sparked the formation of many member clubs around the country. To participate in USDAA trials, dogs must be at least 18 months of age. The USDAA and AKC both offer titles to winning dogs, although the exercises and requirements of the two organizations differ.

Agility trials are a great way to keep your dog active, and they will keep you running, too! You should join a local agility club to learn more about the sport. These clubs offer sessions in which you can introduce your dog to the various obstacles as well as training classes to prepare him for competition. In no time, your dog will be climbing A-frames, crossing the dog walk and flying over hurdles, all with you right beside him. Your heart will leap every time your English Cocker jumps through the hoop—and you'll be having just as much fun (if not more).

FIELD TRIALS

Field trials are offered to the retrievers, pointers and spaniel breeds of the Sporting Group as well as to the Beagles, Dachshunds and Bassets of the Hound Group. The purpose of field trials is to demonstrate a dog's ability to perform his breed's original purpose in the field. The events vary depending on the type of dog, but in all trials dogs compete against one another for placement and for points toward their Field Champion (FC) titles. Dogs that earn their FC titles plus their championships in the conformation ring are known as Dual Champions; this is extremely prestigious, as it shows that the dog is the ideal blend of form and function, excelling in both areas.

Retriever field trials, designed to simulate "an ordinary day's shoot," are popular and likely the most demanding of these trials. Dogs must "mark" the location of downed feathered game and then return the birds to the shooter. Successful dogs are able

A judge's first impression of a dog is the condition of its coat. A shiny coat on a well-groomed dog is eye-catching and indicative of a dog's overall good condition.

to "mark" the downed game by remembering where the bird fell as well as using the wind and terrain. Dogs are tested both on land and in water.

Difficulty levels are based on the number of birds downed as well as the number of "blind retrieves" (where a bird is placed away from the view of the dog and the handler directs the dog by the use of hand signals and verbal commands). The term "Non-Slip" retriever, often applied to these trials, refers to a dog that is steady at the handler's side until commanded to go. Every field trial includes four stakes of increasing levels of difficulty. Each stake is judged by a team of two judges who look for many natural abilities, including steadiness, courage, style, control and training.

HUNTING TESTS

Hunting tests are not competitive like field trials, and participating dogs are judged against a standard, as in a conformation show. The first hunting tests were devised by the North American Hunting Retriever Association (NAHRA) as an alternative to field trials for retriever owners to appreciate their dogs' natural innate ability in the field without the expense and pressure of a formal field trial. The AKC offers hunting tests for spaniels, pointing breeds and retrievers. The intent of hunting tests is the same as that of field trials: to test the dog's ability in a simulated hunting scenario.

The AKC instituted its hunting tests in June 1985; since then, their popularity has grown tremendously. The AKC offers three titles at hunting tests, Junior Hunter (JH), Senior Hunter (SH) and Master Hunter (MH). Each title requires that the dog earn qualifying "legs" at the tests: the JH requiring four; the SH five; and the MH six. In addition to the AKC, the UKC also offers hunting tests through its affiliate club, the Hunting Retriever Club, Inc. (HRC), which began the tests in 1984.

ENGLISH COCKER SPANIEL

You chose your dog because something clicked the minute you set eyes on him. Or perhaps it seemed that the dog selected you and that's what clinched the deal. Either way, you are now investing time and money in this dog, a true pal and an outstanding member of the family. Everything about him is perfect...well, almost perfect. Remember, he is a dog! For that matter, how does he think *you're* doing?

UNDERSTANDING THE CANINE MINDSET

For starters, you and your dog are on different wavelengths. Your dog is similar to a toddler in that both live in the present tense only. A dog's view of life is based primarily on cause and effect. For example, if your dog stumbles down a flight of three steps, the next time he may (hopefully) approach the stairs mroe carefully or he may avoid the steps altogether.

Your dog makes connections based on the fact that he lives in the present, so when he is doing something and you interrupt to dispense praise or a correction, a connection, positive or negative, is made. To the dog, that's like one plus one equals two! In the same sense, it's also easy to see that when your timing is off, you will cause an incorrect connection. The one-plus-one way of thinking is why you must never scold a dog for behavior that

You want your English Cocker always to look up to you as his trusted leader and caregiver.

took place an hour, 15 minutes or even 5 seconds ago. But it is also why, when your timing is perfect, you can teach him to do all kinds of wonderful things— as soon as he has made that essential connection. What helps the process is his desire to please you and to have your approval.

There are behaviors we admire in dogs, such as friendliness and obedience, as well as those behaviors that cause problems to a varying degree. The dog owner who encounters minor behavioral problems is wise to solve them promptly or get professional help. Bad behaviors are not corrected by repeatedly shouting "No" or getting angry with the dog. Only the giving of praise and approval

Socialization at an early age produces pups who are affectionate and welcome attention in return.

for good behavior lets your dog understand right from wrong. The longer a bad behavior is allowed to continue, the harder it is to overcome. A responsible breeder is often able to help. Each dog is unique, so try not to compare your dog's behavior with your neighbor's dog or the one you had as a child.

Have your veterinarian check the dog to see whether a behavior problem could have a physical cause. An earache or toothache, for example, could be the reason for a dog to snap at you if you were to touch his head when putting on his leash. A sharp correction from you would only increase the behavior. When a physical basis is eliminated, and if the problem is not something you understand or can cope with, ask for the name of a behavioral specialist, preferably one who is familiar with the English Cocker Spaniel.

PROFESSIONAL HELP

Every trainer and behaviorist asks, "Why didn't you come to me sooner?" Pet owners often don't want to admit that anything is wrong with their dogs. A dog's problem often is due to the dog and his owner mixing their messages, which will only get worse. Don't put it off; consult a professional to find out whether or not the problem is serious enough to require intervention.

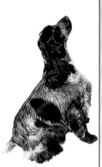

FEAR BITING

The remedy for the fear biter is in the hands of a professional trainer or behaviorist. This is not a behavior that the average pet owner should attempt to correct. However, there are things you should *not* do. Don't sympathize with him, don't pet him and don't, whatever you do, pick him up—you could be bitten in the process, which is even scarier if you bring him up near your face.

Be sure to keep the breeder informed of your progress.

Many things, such as environment and inherited traits, form the basic behavior of a dog, just as in humans. You also must factor into his temperament the purpose for which your dog was originally bred. The major obstacle lies in the dog's inability to explain his behavior to us in a way that we understand. The one thing that you should not do is give up and abandon your dog. Somewhere a misunderstanding has occurred but, with help and patient understanding on your part, you should be able to work out the majority of bothersome behaviors.

AGGRESSION

Although English Cocker Spaniels are very gentle by nature, aggression can occur and then it is a problem. Aggressive behavior is not to be tolerated. It is important to get to the root of the problem to ascertain why the dog is acting in this manner. Aggression is a display of dominance, and the dog should not have the dominant role in his pack, which is, in this case, your family. Have you been firm enough with the puppy or did you accept his dominant behavior because it was so "cute"? Didn't you have time to go to the puppy classes and is this the price you have to pay?

The best solution is to consult a behavioral specialist, one who has experience with the English Cocker Spaniel if possible, rather than trying to handle it yourself with an incorrect approach. Together, perhaps you can pinpoint the cause of your dog's aggression and then do something about it.

BEHAVIOR TOWARD OTHER DOGS

If a dog is aggressive or fearful of another dog, this behavior stems from not enough exposure to other dogs at an early age. It is very important that a puppy learns to trust people and other dogs at a young age through proper socialization. When something or someone frightens the pup, many owners tend to react in a protective way. They pick the puppy up, comfort him and, thus, strengthen his belief that what happened was very scary indeed. If he gets frightened, do not pick him up; instead talk to him in a gentle but firm way and go on as if nothing happened. That way he will learn that, indeed, nothing happened.

DOMINANCE

In the wild, all canines operate on the pack system. Youngsters obey Mom and all older females, and all adult members of the pack obey the top male, who is the leader of the pack. As young males mature, their allegiance shifts from Mom to the "boss man." Pups begin to learn the

---

UNDERSTANDING HOW YOUR DOG TICKS

Dogs do not run on human emotions like love, guilt or spite. They operate on trust and loyalty, or faithfulness, and those are worthy alternatives to what we call love. Dogs don't understand any human language, but they can learn to make connections if all corrections and praise are immediate. If your dog demolished your rug while you were out, that's not guilt you're seeing, but a reaction to your anger. He doesn't know why you're angry, but he knows the boss isn't happy. Dogs are pack animals. They have always lived in a cooperative society. Your dog retains that pack instinct, requiring a leader. You now have that job and the responsibility that goes along with it.

---

rules from the day their eyes and ears open, and they know that breaking the rules brings down the wrath of the pack kings and queens! They also know that there must always be just one leader, and each male has his eye on the position from adolescence. This Alpha system has been effective since the beginning for all pack animals. You can't change it, but you can make it work to your advantage.

All of your training has to impress upon your puppy consistently that you are indeed the "top dog" in his pack. As he matures week after week, you will continue to reinforce that impression. Dogs are patiently cunning, and your dog will wait for the precise moment when you let down your guard and then wham! he will take over. If you let him, that is.

Keeping dominance under control is in your hands. Good-natured, gentle but firm, consistent training is the answer. Positive reinforcement will yield positive results. Correct poor or unwanted behavior by directing your dog into desirable behavior (via treats, distractions and obedience commands) and you will have turned a negative into a positive. Not too hard, but it takes patience to stay ahead of an exceptionally dominant dog. On the other hand, such a dog can be a lot of fun if you

LOOK AT ME WHEN I SPEAK TO YOU

Your dog considers direct eye contact as a sign of dominance. A shy dog will avoid looking at you; a dominant dog will try to stare you down. What you want is for your dog to pay attention when you speak, and that doesn't necessarily involve direct eye contact. In dealing with a problem dog, avert your gaze momentarily, return to face the dog and give an immediate down command. Show him that you're the boss.

appreciate the challenge. Seeing through the ways in which he tries to outwit your leadership is thoroughly amusing. It would seem that dogs were the original "con artists." They will figure out how to trick you into doing what they want. How often do you fall for a sudden bark at the door, only to find that no one is there, and return to discover that the dog has taken your chair? Or how about when he asks to go out and instead leads you to the cookie jar? How many times has a favorite toy been dropped expectantly in your lap? Dog language it may be, but it's pretty smart!

Veterinarians can suffer bites from dogs that are terrified of being put on the examination table; this is the dog's way of taking control of a situation in which he feels vulnerable. So putting your dog onto a grooming table (or a work bench or even a picnic table) for weekly grooming is another subtle way of telling him that you are in charge. At first the dog may find it a bit unsettling to be up off the ground on a small platform. However, once he knows he's safe and accepts that this is the place for routine brushing and combing, he won't have any fear or feelings of aggression when put onto the table at the vet's.

SEPARATION ANXIETY

Any behaviorist will tell you that separation anxiety is the most common problem about which pet owners complain. It is also one of the easiest to prevent. Unfortunately, a behaviorist usually is not consulted until the dog is a stressed-out, neurotic mess. At that stage, it is indeed a problem that requires the help of a professional.

Training the puppy to the fact that people in the house come and go is essential in order to avoid this anxiety. Leaving the puppy in his crate or a confined area while family members go in and out, and stay out for longer and longer periods of time, is the basic way to desensitize the pup to the family's frequent departures. If you are at home most of every day, make it a point to go out for at least an hour or two whenever possible.

How you leave is vital to the dog's reaction. Your dog is no fool. He knows the difference between sweats and business suits, jeans and dresses. He sees you pat your pocket to check for your wallet, open your briefcase, check that you have your cell

Rub any English Cocker's tummy and watch him smile!

I CAN'T SMILE WITHOUT YOU

How can you tell whether your dog is suffering from separation anxiety? Not every dog who enjoys a close bond with his owner will suffer from separation anxiety. In actuality, only a small percentage of dogs are affected. Separation anxiety manifests itself in dogs older than one year of age and may not occur until the dog is a senior. A number of destructive behaviors are associated with the problem, including scratch marks in front of doorways, bite marks on furniture, drool stains on furniture and flooring and tattered draperies, carpets or cushions. The most reliable sign of separation anxiety is howling and crying when the owner leaves and then barking like mad for extended periods. Affected dogs may also defecate or urinate throughout the home, attempt to escape when the door opens, vocalize excessively and show signs of depression (including loss of appetite, listlessness and lack of activity).

phone or pick up the car keys. He knows from the hurry of the kids in the morning that they're off to school until afternoon. Lipstick? Aftershave lotion? Lunch boxes? Every move you make registers in his sensory perception and memory. Your puppy knows more about your departures than you do. You can't get away with a thing!

Before you got dressed, you checked the dog's water bowl and his supply of toys (make sure that they are durable, long-lasting toys), and you turned the radio on low. You will leave him in what he considers his "safe" area, not with total freedom of the house. If you've invested in child safety gates, you can be reasonably sure that he'll remain in the designated area. Don't give him access to a window where he can watch you leave the house. If you're leaving for only an hour or two, just put him into his crate with a safe toy.

THE MACHO DOG

The Venus/Mars differences are found in dogs, too. Males have distinct behaviors that, while seemingly sex-related, are more closely connected to the role of the male as leader. Marking territory by urinating on it is one means that male dogs use to establish their presence. Doing so merely says, "I've been here." Small dogs often attempt to lift their legs higher on the tree than the previous male. While this is natural behavior outdoors on items like telephone poles, fence posts, fire hydrants and most other upright objects, marking indoors is totally unacceptable. Treat it as you would a house-training accident and clean thoroughly to eradicate the scent.

Another behavior often seen in the macho male, mounting is a dominance display. Neutering the dog before six months of age helps to deter this behavior. You can discourage him from mounting by catching the dog as he's about to mount you, stepping quickly aside and saying "Off!"

Now comes the test! You are ready to walk out the door. Do not give your English Cocker Spaniel a big hug and a fond farewell. Do not drag out a long goodbye. Those are the very things that jump-start separation anxiety. Toss a biscuit into the dog's area, call out "So long, pooch" and close the door. You're gone. The chances are that the dog may bark a couple of times, or maybe whine once or twice, and then settle down to enjoy his biscuit and take a lovely nap, especially if you took him for a nice long walk after breakfast. As he grows up, the barks and whines will stop because it's an old routine, so why should he make the effort?

When you first brought home the puppy, the come-and-go routine was intermittent and constant. He was put into his crate with a tiny treat. You left (silently) and returned in 3 minutes, then 5, then 10, then 15, then half an hour, until finally you could leave without a problem and be gone for 2 or 3 hours. If, at any time in the future, there's a "separation" problem, refresh his memory by going back to that basic training.

Now comes the next most important part—your return. Do not make a big production of coming home. "Hi, poochie" is as grand a greeting as he needs. When you've taken off your hat and coat, tossed your briefcase on the hall table and glanced at the mail, and the dog has settled down from the excitement of seeing you "in person" from his confined area, then go and give him a warm, friendly greeting. A potty trip is needed and a walk would be appreciated, since he's been such a good dog.

CHEWING

All puppies chew. All dogs chew. This is a fact of life for canines, and sometimes you may think it's what your dog does best! A pup starts chewing when his first set of teeth erupts and continues throughout the teething period. Chewing gives the pup relief from itchy gums and incoming teeth and, from that time on, he gets great satisfaction out of this normal,

It's normal for puppies to experience a type of separation anxiety when taken from their siblings to go to new homes. With your love and attention, your new puppy will soon feel at home with you.

somewhat idle, canine activity. Providing safe chew toys is the best way to direct this behavior in an appropriate manner. Chew toys are available in all sizes, textures and flavors, but you must monitor the wear-and-tear inflicted on your pup's toys to be sure that the ones you've chosen are safe and remain in good condition.

Puppies cannot distinguish between a rawhide toy and a nice leather shoe or wallet. It's up to you to keep your possessions away from the dog and to keep your eye on the dog. There's a form of destruction caused by chewing that is not the dog's fault. Let's say you allow him on the sofa. One day he takes a rawhide bone up on the sofa and, in the course of chewing on the bone, takes up a bit of fabric. He continues to chew. Disaster! Now you've learned the lesson: dogs with chew toys have to be either kept

GIMME WHEELS!

Chasing cars or bikes is dangerous for all parties concerned: dogs, drivers and cyclists. Something about those wheels going around fascinates dogs, but that fascination can end in disastrous results. Corrections for your dog's chasing behavior must be immediate and firm. Tell him "Leave it!" and then give him either a sit or a down command. Get kids on bikes to help saturate your dog with spinning wheels while he politely practices his sits and downs.

It takes time for an English Cocker pup to grow into his bark. Begin "Quiet" training from the first yip.

off furniture and carpets, carefully supervised or put into their confined areas for chew time.

The wooden legs of furniture are favorite objects for chewing. The first time, tell the dog "Leave it!" (or "No!") and offer him a chew toy as a substitute. But your clever dog may be hiding under the chair and doing some silent destruction, which you may not notice until it's too late. In this case, it's time to try one of the foul-tasting products, made specifically to prevent destructive chewing, that is sprayed on the objects of your dog's chewing attention. These products also work to keep the dog away from plants, trash, etc. It's even a good way to stop the dog from "mouthing" or chewing on your hands or the leg of your pants. (Be sure to wash your hands after the mouthing lesson!) A little spray goes a long way.

BARKING

Here's a big, noisy problem! Telling a dog he must never bark is like telling a child not to speak! Consider how confusing it must be to your dog that you are using your voice (which is your form of barking) to teach him when to bark and when not to! That is precisely the reason not to "bark back" when the dog's barking is annoying you (or your neighbors). Try to understand the scenario from the dog's viewpoint. He barks. You bark. He barks again, you bark again. This "conversation" can go on forever!

The first time your adorable little puppy said "Yip" or "Yap, you were ecstatic. His first word! You smiled, you told him how smart he was—and you allowed him to do it. So there's that one-plus-one thing again, because he will understand by your happy reaction that "Mr. Alpha loves it when I talk."

> ## THE TOP-DOG TUG
> When puppies play tug-of-war, the dominant pup wins. Children also play this kind of game but, for their own safety, must be prevented from ever engaging in this type of play with their dogs. Playing tug-o-war games can result in a dog's developing aggressive behavior. Don't be the cause of such behavior.

Ignore his barking in the beginning, and allow it, but don't encourage barking during play. Instead, use the "put a toy in it" method to tone it down. Add a very soft "Quiet" as you hand off the toy. If the barking continues, stand up straight, fold your arms and turn your back on the dog. If he barks, you won't play, and you should follow the same rule for all undesirable behavior during play.

Dogs bark in reaction to sounds and sights. Another dog's bark, a person passing by or even just rustling leaves can set off a barker. If someone coming up your driveway or to your door provokes a barking frenzy, use the saturation method to stop it. Have several friends come and go every three or four minutes over as long a period of time as they can spare (it could take a couple of hours). Attach about a foot of rope to the dog's collar and have very small treats handy. Each time a car pulls up or a person approaches, let the dog bark once (grab the rope if you need to physically restrain him), say "Okay, good dog," give him a treat and make him sit. "Okay" is the release command. It lets the dog know that he has alerted you and tells him that you are now in charge. That person leaves and the next arrives, and so on and so on

FOUR ON THE FLOOR
You must discourage your dog from jumping up to get attention or for any other reason. To do so, bump the jumper gently with your hip as you turn away. "Four on the floor" requires praise. Once the dog sits on command, prevent him from attempting to jump again by asking him to sit-stay before petting him. Back away if he breaks the sit.

until everyone—especially the dog—is bored and the barking has stopped. Don't forget to thank your friends. Your neighbors, by the way, may be more than willing to assist you in this parlor game if it means a

DIGGING OUT

Some dogs love to dig. Others wouldn't think of it. Digging is considered "self-rewarding behavior" because it's fun! Of all the digging solutions offered by the experts, most are only marginally successful and none is guaranteed to work. The best cure is prevention, which means removing the dog from the offending site when he digs as well as distracting him when you catch him digging so that he turns his attentions elsewhere. That means that you have to supervise your dog's yard time. An unsupervised digger can create havoc with your landscaping or, worse, run away!

quiet dog on the block.

Excessive barking outdoors is more difficult to keep in check because, when it happens, he is outside and you are probably inside. A few warning barks are fine, but use the same method to tell him when enough

is enough. You will have to stay outside with him for that bit of training.

There is one more kind of vocalizing which is called "idiot barking" (from idiopathic, meaning of unknown cause). It is usually rhythmic or a timed series of barks. Put a stop to it immediately by calling the dog to come. This form of barking can drive neighbors crazy and commonly occurs when a dog is left outside at night or for long periods of time during the day. He is completely and thoroughly bored! A change of scenery may help, such as relocating him to a room indoors when he is used to being outside. A few new toys or different dog biscuits might be the solution. If he is left alone and no one can get home during the day, a noontime walk with a local dog-sitter would be the perfect solution.

BEGGING

We're not talking about eating, diets or nutrition here, we're talking about bad habits. Face it. All dogs are beggars. Food is the motivation for everything we want our dogs to do and, when you combine that with their innate ability to "con" us in order to get their way, it's a wonder there aren't far more obese dogs in the world.

Who can resist the bleeding-heart look that says "I'm

Your English Cocker should always have the opportunity to relieve himself in the appropriate place so that he will never have to be confined in close quarters with an "accident."

taught your dog. Use "Off" for the pawing. A sit or even a long down will interrupt the whining. His reward in these situations is definitely not a treat! Casual verbal praise is enough. Be sure all members of the family follow the same rules. There is a different type of begging that does demand your immediate response and that is the appeal to be let (or taken) outside! Usually that is a quick paw or small whine to get your attention, followed by a race to the door. This type of begging needs your quick attention and approval. Of course, a really smart dog will soon figure out how to cut you off at the pass and direct you to that cookie jar on your way to the door! Some dogs are always one step ahead of us.

starving," or the paw that gently pats your knee while its owner gives you a knowing look, or the whining "please" or even the total body language of a perfect sit beneath the cookie jar. No one who professes to love his dog can turn down the pleas of his clever canine's performances every time. One thing is for sure, though: definitely do not allow begging at the table. Family meals do not include your dog.

Control your dog's begging habit by making your dog work for his rewards. Ignore his begging when you can. Utilize the obedience commands you've

Adopting an English Cocker into your family is a serious undertaking. You owe it to your new trusting puppy to provide him with the very best for his whole life.

INDEX

My English Cocker Spaniel

PUT YOUR PUPPY'S FIRST PICTURE HERE

Dog's Name _____

Date _____ Photographer _____